All
Poetry

All Poetry

Paulo Leminski

Translated by
Charles A. Perrone
and
Ivan Justen Santana

NEW LONDON LIBRARIUM

All Poetry
by Paulo Leminski
Original Title: *Toda Poesia*

Translated by Charles A. Perrone and Ivan Justen Santana
Edited by Ana Lessa-Schmidt

Cover design by Elisa von Randow
Interior artwork by Marco Mazzarotto.

Published by
New London Librarium
Hanover, CT 06350 – USA
NLLibrarium.com

ISBNs
Hardcover: 978-1-947074-64-4
Paperback: 978-1-947074-65-1

Contents

Presentation

In the Brazilian arts of the late twentieth century and early twenty-first century, Paulo Leminski (1944-1989) stands as a singular and widely celebrated figure. In addition to poetry, he wrote experimental narrative, biographies, creative essays, songs (words + music), and lyrics. He was a polyglot translator, tutor-teacher, advertising man, and judoka. In the 1980s he was one of the leading poets of his generation. Decades later, his complete poems would become the best seller in all of Brazil (for books other than non-fiction), quite a rare achievement for a volume of verse, and nine years out it has sold over 200,000 copies. It is a pleasure to bring a full translation of that collection in Portuguese to English-language readerships.

The foreword of the source volume (*Toda Poesia*, 2013) was written by poet Alice Ruiz, spouse of Leminski for twenty years and mother of their three children.

For further information and explanation of the present collected whole poetry of Paulo Leminski, see the translators' afterword following the body of the text.

Acknowledgements

For suggestions, assistance, information, encouragement and/or collegiality, the translators would like to thank Anna Klobucka, Paulo Henriques Britto, Rodrigo Garcia Lopes, Ricardo Sternberg, Antonio Carlos Secchin, William Allegrezza, Sean Negus, Christopher Dunn, André Vallias, Charles Bernstein, Marco Mazzarotto, who designed the cover and the interior artwork, and all those around the world who responded to an inquiry about the lead poem of *La vie en close*. Above all, recognition is due to Aurea Leminski, manager of the literary estate, for the initiative to bring this Anglophone volume of her father's poems to fruition.

Foreword

This book is above all an entire life of poetry. A life totally dedicated to poetic making. Short, it's true, but intense, fruitful, and original.

It's better to leave the critical analyses to the specialists. Here it's up to me to remember the history / life of the books that make up this unique book.

One of Paulo's earliest poems, perhaps the very first, was written in Latin, during his initial adolescence, when he was studying at the Paraná Catholic Boarding School. That precocious co-existence with clergy gave him impetus to seek further cloistered life, more for the facilitated retreat, so opportune for the study of the movement of the soul and the wealth of words, than for religious faith, properly speaking. Not that it was not present, but there was also a virile energy, the kind that makes us want to conquer the world and absorb what it has to teach us. Thus, the cloister did not last long, like any flighty adolescent idea, but it was enough to sprout roots, for the love of knowledge, once awoken, is not easily erased.

The first time I saw Paulo was at the awards ceremony of a poetry contest in Curitiba. All the prize-winning poems were read by their authors, and his was the only one that, for me, had something forceful and innovative to say. Such an original diction must have been beyond the jury's ability to appreciate, back then, but that impeccably constructed poem could not be overlooked. But the one that should have been awarded first place received only an honorable mention. Time would correct that mistake, as the top-prize winners of that contest are today in no special place, quite a difference from him.

Four years later some girlfriends took me to his twenty-fourth birthday party.

The first thing we discussed was poetry. The last as well.

We spent most of the party in his office, and I was nearly buried by a profusion of words, ideas, and projects ([his experimental novel] *Catatau*, for example, had a mere eight pages and was still called Descartes com lentes [with lenses]). We talked about authors we both admired, and he introduced me to haiku-ists and the concrete poets, of whom I was unaware. Meanwhile, I, recently returned from a two-year stint in Rio de Janeiro, showed him the newest (in all senses) in Brazilian popular music, particularly *tropicalismo*, which had yet to reach him.

Like love, poetry and music grew and grew in our life in common.

In 1976 when the photographer Jack Pires came to us with a proposal to do a book together with Paulo, we spread his photos on the floor and began to search for the shortest poems that could converse or rhyme with those images. That's how the first publication of a very small part of his poetry was born: *forty clicks in curitiba.*

Next in turn, 1980, was *were it not this and it would be less were it not so much and it would be almost,* a splendid volume, initiative and gift of two friends, Márcio Santos and Nego Miranda, owners of the portrait studio ZAP, who did photographic enlargements of the typescripts of his 1940s' Remington. The printing was made possible via barters with partner graphics outfits.

Paulo soaked up the idea of exchange and used it to be able to produce, in the same year, his third "independent" book of poems: *Polonaises*. A homage to his roots, in the typeface of Solidarity, a revolutionary workers' movement led by Lech Valesa which was happening in Poland at the time.

One of the problems of self-produced editions was deciding what to do with the complete print runs, which stayed with the authors. In 1983, our house was overrun with more than a 1000 copies of each of those three books, in addition to the volumes of *Catatau* (also an author's imprint) and my own two books, all restricted to the local Curitiba market (we did not sell them, we gifted them to friends). Then we found out that the publishing house Brasiliense also had a bookstore in São Paulo where one could put up for sale books crafted "outside the axis" [the São Paulo - Rio de Janeiro circuit].

We sent a copy of each book to Luiz Schwarcz, at the time the right-hand man of [owner] Caio Graco Prado, responsible for innovative series such as Encanto [Enchantment] Radical, Primeiros Passos [First steps], and others. Luiz called to thank us and asked if we had further unpublished works, since new material would give more life to the collection of the extant ones. Thus was born the first nation-wide release for each of us.

Caprices & re-laxities was the name that Paulo devised to gather those first poems, in which there is a gamesome bias, but without shirking rigor. A name denounces and prescribes, at the same time. The book appeared in 1983.

Next came *Distracted we shall overcome* (1987). The name remits, in a certain way, to the previous book, apparently with a chunk of hope, although the tenor of the poems suggests greater skepticism.

Paulo began to choose from the subsequent output based on a fresh criterion, or better said, displaying a new style that was taking shape. What he called "Parnassian chic" would go into *La vie en close*, and the rest, still without a defined place, went to a folder that he baptized as "The Ex-Stranger," a book that he would think about later. Except there was no later, and that was foretold in the titles he chose. The "stranger", which is how the poet feels in the practical world, would soon be "ex-". And the life that was finally en/closing seems to come into focus, highlight just what is essential: la vie en close.

I watched the selection process closely; once it was complete, he asked me to take care of his unpublished items and he put me in charge of directing them to Caio and/or Luiz, in case he (Paulo) did not have enough time. Caio published *La vie en close*. Samuel Leon, of the Iluminuras house, in addition to the prose, published *The Ex-Stranger* and *Winterverno*, a book with very short poems by Paulo and images by João Virmond Suplicy Neto. And now [2013] all the poetry returns to the hands of Luiz Schwarcz of Companhia das Letras.

These books are different from each other, but they all bear the same mark of poetic scripture. Roots in concrete poetry and synthesis, in experimentation and the colloquial. The same commitment to two apparently mutually exclusive things: innovation and eagerness to communicate, to say. Saying replete with a consciousness of the necessity for silence. Perhaps for those and other reasons his poetry continues to be so current yet conversant with the future.

And now, finally brought together, it can offer a complete view of what poetry was for Leminski and Leminski for poetry.*

ALICE RUIZ S.

*(Here, the sum total of all verses previously published in books)

I. forty clicks in curitiba

[1976]

Spoiling for a fight with it all
Giant in vain
Against the white wall
He nails the palm of his hand

•

A single lifetime is short
for more than one dream

•

Will I myself need
to explain
Mona Lisa´s smile
in order for you
to pay heed
when I say
that time goes by?

•

the criterion
"way off the rails"
will not serve
to condemn people
these creatures
full of entrails

•

How I wish I had
one of those treasure maps
to lead me to an old trunk
full of treasure maps

•

Closing bodies with spells
like one closing a book
known by heart so well.

Spell-closing to the bone
like one closing a book
in an unknown language
and once unknown the body
everything else is unknown.

Only an old man
to discover,
behind a single stone,
the entirety of spring.

All time goes walking.
Should it stop,
its companion will be
a single line
once upon a time
once upon a time
once upon a time

Sunday
The little birdies tweet
Sweet enough to put in coffee

People who keep
birds in cages
have heartfelt vocations.
The birds are kept safe
from any salvation.

People on every block.
Six o'clock.
Hot food on coals.
Casseroles.

I've spent hours hesitating
before killing the creature.
After all,
it was a creature like me,
with rights,
with duties.
And, above all,
incapable of killing a creature,
like me.

Think fast.
What passed?
Who's coming?
Ugly or becoming?
Not a soul.

the sharp teeth of life
prefer meat
in the most tender youth
when
bites hurt more
and leave indelible scars
when
the taste of meat
has yet to be spoiled
by the day-to-day brine

that's when
one still cries
that's when
one still rebels
that's when
still

●

twisted body
against the cold
sack on back - empty
are you stealing the wind?

●

Friend
Enemy
I had nothing with the sea
Nor it with me
I was a man of drought
Today put out to dry
In this here alley

The ousted eye sees
what yours do not.
You, seeing others,
think that it´s me?
Or with all you see
do you think it's you?

Fruits that only ripen
After plucked off the vine
Old acquaintances of mine

The rain has stopped
Folks get their steps wet
The heavy streets

this?
right here?
already?
like this?

Loving,
enhanced up to
two thousand times
is the size.

After today
life will never be the same
unless I insist on deceiving myself
actually
after yesterday
that's the way it was
the day before yesterday
before
tomorrow

is this
by any chance
a place
to toss shadows?

someone who's alive
always arrives at the
wrong time at last
to say present
when nobody asked

●

silence
sets out to mistreat me
by dictating
abbreviations of myself
and,
maybe,
dilating my very own self

●

some protect themselves
behind
a barrier
of good mornings
good afternoons
good nights
so as not to have
to see what's going on

●

How does night become day?
The day become night?
Only through seeing.
Everything we know.

the time
between the blowing
and the candle being out

To scout
the door they forgot to shut.
The alley with a clear way out.
The door with no key cut.
Life.

Time at every turn
seems to be
retarding
and me
reading
reading
reading
will end up turning
into a legend

They're gonna kill me in the street.
When someone says out loud,
mainly,
that I belong to the crowd
who thinks that the street
is the main part of the city.

suddenly I discovered
I don't say America or gunpowder
work of so many
an account in the red
standing on tiptoes
besides the noble exercise
the wisest measure read
in life to get ahead

this day
this perverse day
that came after yesterday

II. caprices & re-laxities

[1983]

Here, poems to read, in silence,
the eyes, the heart and intelligence.
Poems to read out loud.
Poems, song texts, lyrics, to sing.
Which are which, that's up to you, partner.

caprices & re-laxities

(insights, pick-ups, touch-ups & shocks)

    of how
    the polack jan korneziowsky
    put on the persona/costume
    of joseph conrad
    and turned into lord jim /childe harold

one of these days i want to be
a great english poet
from centuries ago
and say oh heaven, oh sea,
oh clan, oh destiny on deck
to fight in india in 1866 and
disappear in a clandestine shipwreck

●

counternarcissus

in myself
i see the other
and another
and another
ultimately dozens
trains passing
wagons full of people
hundreds of cousins

the other
who's there in me
is you
you
and you

just as
i am in you
i am in him
and in us
and only when
we´re on our own
will we be at peace
even if we´re alone

the p that's
in the poky &
hides itself
i know y

i just don't know
where neither and

over the empty table
i unfold a clean cloth
the mind calm and stable
the word cute and able

here ends the flight
of the rageful night
that wanted in no way
to be recast as pure day

we are another
a god, at last,
is back where we started

friday sounds the same as basket

may they be clean
the linens of this friday
the linens in the basket

may it be your party day
a full basket
                like a moon
all made of full moons

in the glimmering
        white
your love
        your hate
                simmering
                        display

your pomp
so many parties
so many clothes
                in the basket
                        full
                                of friday

may they be clean
the linens of this friday
may it be your day to party and romp

even
at the age
of becoming
myself

i still
mistake
a happy stage
for this
quiet rage

•

staring
into someone´s eyes
i know if that person
is hip to things
or not

one who is not
just cannot hold
a stare for long

from the center of my acme
this poem stares at me

•

disassembling frevo

disassembling
this plaything
i discovered
that frevo
has a lot to do
with a certain
mestizo way of being
a mixed way vat
of wanting
this and that
without ever being flat
due to this
nor to that

of being a half
and half a being
without refraining
from being whole
and even so
not giving up
on being a complete
mystery

i want to chase
the january
that ends the race
in february
doing the frevo
that i embrace
arriving to the front
in first place

birds
    from branch above
        to branch below

my thinking
    from rhyme
        to rhyme
          wanders

until one
    that says
        i love you

of the things
i did by the meter
everyone will plot
how many kilometers
were wrought

those
in centimeters
minimal sentiments
infinite impulses
will they not?

african

giraffes

like my

grandparents

oh how i long to

see the world

from heights

as you do

Who is born with a heart?
A heart must be made.
I've had quite the part
In making my chest shade.

With that may no one be born.
A heart is one rare hunk
That we find one fair morn
And we'd better get drunk.

i'm not the silence
that means to say words
or to clap its hands
for performances of chance

i'm a river of words
i request a moment of silences
pauses waltzes wandering scrolls
and a bit of forgetfulness

just one and i can leave this space
and star in that theater
called time

〰

my mother would say

- boil, water!
- fry, egg!
- drip, faucet!

and all would obey

this
all
is
alice

if alice
saw herself there
all that alice saw
she dare not say

if there
one were to say
the words that act
yet not in her way

there
right there
inside alice
only alice
with alice
has her exact sway

nothing so common
that i can't call it
mine

nothing so mine
i can't say it's ours
alone

nothing so soft
that i can't say it's
a bone

nothing so hard
that can't be said
and done

gotta stop writing
notes of congratulations
as if i were camöens
and the iliads of my days
were lusiads,
rosas, vieiras, rogations

Good day, elderly bards.
Leave in my mouth
the taste of verses
stronger than I will ever make.

The eve will come when I know them
so well that I'll quote them to you
as one who has made
them a little too,
believe me.

●

dry that off

see if you can spy

this tear
that i shed

examine

examine closely

see if it is not
water from the stone
gold from the mine
this drop of water

this master-
piece of mine

the sonnet the chronicle the acrostic
the fear of forgetfulness
the vice of feeling everything in gear
and these days
long days like years
yes i practice all
the provincial genres

●

day
to the cousin bird

was it you
that showed up to chirp
yesterday
just before
sunrise?

or was it
perhaps
an aunt a sister a brother
a voice
already
so
faraway
that this day
even seems to be another?

●

I threw my severed
Head at your window
Moonlit night
Wide open window

It knocks on the wall
Losing its teeth
Falling on the bed
Heavy with thoughts

It may startle you
You may behold it
Against the moon
After the color of my eyes

Maybe you'll use it
As an alarm clock
On the bedside table

I don't want to startle you
I only ask for decent treatment
For this sudden head
On my part

the tree is a poem
it's not there
to be worth it

it's there
in the wind that might teem
in the sun that might cream
in the moon potential diadem

it's only there

●

what do i care
twelve past noon
may time strike
in these clocks

a matter of tic-tac
for me now
it's a quarter to four
or two twenty-one

nineteen and eighteen
apart
for eleven thirty
only my heart

●

nothing the sun
couldn't explain

everything the moon
more chic by the hour

there is no rain
to fade this flower

❧

i don't lament
the loss of smell
after all it's
only for acts of sniffing
the four elements
let's get to the facts

i lost the palate
but just because i lost it
did i remove from my head
the taste of pineapple

i don't forget the ears
for having commenced
the war of the senses
i turned to silence
as sound makes no sense

a consequence
takes me over
as if i were getting high

❧

there is a planet
lost in a fold
of the solar system

there it's easy to mistake
smiling for screaming

it's hard to distinguish
this planet from dreaming

object
of my most desperate desire
do not be the one
i cannot see though i'm on fire

be the star kissing me prior
an orient that inspires me
indigo loving grace

do anything for me
but for heaven's sake
or for the two of us
just be

i don't believe
that dante's pain
was greater than
this dental pain
that i shall feel
from this
day on

i don't believe
that joyce
saw more in a word
than what might be heard
that in this pasargada
is interred

nor do i believe
that mallarmé
saw more
than this eye
in this mirror
now
never
sees me

The empty vagina
imagines
that the page (with no vaseline)
fills it in and
plagiarizes her own self

This tongue that i always speak
(and always sprick)
and distracted i write
although not so frequently
bankrupt estate
collapses on paper
                              when i drool
and finished in a text
i finish

business man
make as many business
as you can
you will never know
who i am

your mother
says no
your father
says never

you'll never know
how the strawberry fields
it will be forever

                              [originally written in English]

legends landing here
from lovely lands
of lapsed orients

make my happiness happen
as this life does not

a letter an ember throughout
within the text
cloud full of my rain
crosses the desert for me
the mountain walks on
the sea between the two
a syllable a sob
a yes a no a sigh
signs saying we
when we no longer are

four days not seeing you
and you haven't changed a bit

need some sugar in the lemonade

from my sweetheart i have strayed

i've swum and swum yet no progress have i made

always the same crummy poet
wasting time with humankind

my friend
so hesitant
deals with things
semifusas

when confused
even the exact
medusas
are transmuted
into muses

ও

knowing
that by saying so
- poem -
i was killing you
even so
i told you

knowing
that by doing so
you were lasting
it was hard
even so
i brought you

even so
i made you
though i knew you
fleeting
an unhappy soul
always unhappy

even so
i desired you more
even knowing
that i'd want you
and without answer
i'd ask for an encore

∾

between external debt
and internal doubt
my commercial
heart
        alternates

pomp for so long all defeats
caution so poorly calculated
  pause on the agenda
maybe in chirps set on seats
  passing me this mid-day
crosses these streets
  placates in light
the cause of this dawn

  calm provokes me
in anger and war does flourish
  all this longing my soul
so much waltz flame nostalgia
  so much A so much B so much Z

so much me may look to me like you

may so much distance
between us not compete
with this sun
that now fleets
between one wave
and another wave
in the ocean of sheets

friday,
sixth day of the week,
ash-grey

how many times
will you be thirteen?

how many hours
have your months?

how many thursdays,
fifth day,
will be thirty?

how many mondays,
second day,
are not even never?

how many wednesdays,
fourth day,
infinite?

you alice me
i´m entirely enticed
wings
   all of them winged
over lettuce-colored ices
there
  yes
    i´d lose my vises

when i make it to seventy
this adolescence will be ended

i'll give up this crazy life
and be a tenured faculty member

i'll do what my father wants
to begin life with perfect pitch

i'll do what my mother wishes
and seize every opportunity
to become a pillar of society
and scratch my law school itch

then see everything in sane conscience
at the end of this adolescence

may this illusion
not fade away

you're allowing
that illusion
to stay
just like this

i dismiss
you
from my play

what's new
shocks me no more
nothing new
under the sun

just the same
eternal egg
hatches the same newness

petals
drop not this dew

eyes
lose not those tears

auras already gone
grateful for the grace
the grace that i find
in all that remains
for everything's apace

he dealt
just an L
and she Ah
she was there
under the pelt
as one who only
H

to love an A
like an L
who can tell?

So sorry, dear chair,
you're stepping on my foot.
This way you look more like
that table: all it does
is to tire my beauty.

You two are going to see something.
Just because it's made of iron,
this nail, the hammer
can't grind my finger.

You two have no head at all.
You're nothing but objects.
You'll never know
how much homesickness hurts
when what was once close-by
has become what's faraway.

So sorry, dear chair,
you're stepping on my foot.
This way you look more like
that table: all it does
is to tire my beauty.

As for the rest - goodbye.

ᕕ

they when they come
they when they go
lines not even some
lines not even no
i care not to gain
they do it themselves
as if it were in vain

they when they go
they when they come
poetry that yes
seems not even so

my 7 falls

upon my first fall
a parachute stall

i went like stone thrall
into my second fall

from second to third fall
was a leap like silk shawl

and then a fifth fall
takes the fourth onto a pall

in the sixth i kept falling
and now, excuse me
another abyss comes calling

how i wish a vulture
would devour my heart!
a slice of raw meat
to eat at the food cart!

how i wish an apache
would reap my scalp!
may this time no disguise
manage to depart!

hopefully a hurricane
will befall my ship!
let no god or dragon
loosen my grip!

&

in matters
of tact
    my dear boy
i've got something neat

if you wish
i´ve even got
a fate
    at my feet

flowers
are really
ungrateful

we pick them
then they die
without further ado
as if between us
there had never
been venus

sure history makes sense
i read this in a dense old book
   that was such an ambiguous blend
it's long gone in the hands of some friend

   we will soon reach the conclusion
that it was all a hack without knack
   and we will come back
to the usual confusion

polonaises

Polały się łzy me czyste, rzęsiste,
Na me dzieciństwo sielskie, anielskie,
Na moją młodość górną i durną,
Na mój wiek męski, wiek klęski.
Polały sie łzy me czyste, rzęsiste...

[1839]

Choveram-me lágrimas limpas, ininterruptas,
Na minha infância campestre, celeste,
Na mocidade de alturas e loucuras,
Na minha idade adulta, idade de desdita;
Choveram-me lágrimas limpas, ininterruptas...

[1979]

adam mickiewicz
translated from polish to portuguese by
p leminski

Clean tears rained on me, uninterrupted,
In my childhood, agrestial, celestial,
In my youth of heights and follies,
In my adult age, age so distressful;
Clean tears rained on me, uninterrupted...

[2021]

old leon and natalia in coyoacan

this time it won't be snowing as in petrograd that day
the sky will be clear and the sun will be shining
you sleeping and me dreaming

neither coats nor cossacks as in petrograd that day
only you naked and me as i was born
me sleeping and you dreaming

there won't be shouting crowds as in petrograd that day
silence us two blue murmurs
me and you sleeping and dreaming

there will never be another day as in petrograd that day
nothing like a day departing after another coming
you and me dreaming and sleeping

rain dance

dear miss rainfall
may I have the honor
of the next dance
and let's go wander
through these fields
to the sound of this rain
falling on the keyboard

here

on this rock

someone sat down
to spy the sea

the sea
didn't stop
to be spied

it was sea
on every other side

●

a god is also the wind
seen only in his effects
panicking trees
banners
trembling waters
ships off to the races
oh teach me
to suffer out of sight
to enjoy in silence
my own transient pace
never twice
in the same place

to this god
who raises dust on the highways
leading them to chase
i consecrate this sigh

may it grow within
'til it becomes a great gale

a little bird
comes back to the tree
that's no longer had

my thoughts
fly to you
just to be sad

i've been feeling bland

i raise my hand
it's the hand of a monkey

i've been feeling lonely
just knowing i'm only dust

i've been walking to taint
a devil aspires to be a saint

i've spanned the whole arc
the glass at halfway mark

i've been living fatherless

i don't believe in highways
but indeed there are
            nevertheless

                    [last three lines originally written in Spanish]

one day
we were going to be homer
our work no less than an iliad

then later
the going getting rougher
maybe you could be a rimbaud
an ungaretti some fernando pessoa
a lorca an éluard a ginsberg

finally
we ended up the small provincial poet
we'd always been
behind so many masks
that time treated like flowers

a poem
that's not understood
is worthy of note

supreme dignity
of a boat
drifting off course

My grandfather-monkey
The one that Darwin pursued
Looks at me from the branch:
He looks for canine strength
The vigor of all pulses
The panting chest
The shaking of the head
Labor's length

Everything is gone

Nothing remains
Of the primate thrill
Of the oxen brawn

To know
To know will kill

spacetimeship for alice

frag
  ments
    of the shipwreck
        of life
thrown
  onto the beach
    of an unknown land
reasons for
    us to reach
          out so
      to hold
        so tight
together to face
    the night
      of interstellar spaces

two madmen in the neighborhood

one spends his days
kicking posts to see if they light up

the other his nights
erasing words
against blank paper

every neighborhood has a madman
whom it treats sympathetically well
it's just a question of time
for me to be treated as well

the wind blows i move
again the wind does blow
i'm back moving again
always around this love
of mine for the wind

nothing was dutiful
like what was dreamed
but it was welcome
as if everything
were beautiful

for freedom and struggle

please bury me with the trotskyists
in the common grave of the idealists
where lie in peace those
whom power corrupted not

with my heart bury me
in river-bank fashion
where the hurt injured knee
touched petrified passion

my polish heart returned
a heart that my grandfather
brought from far away for me
a crushed heart
a trampled heart
the heart of a poet

dark the road
dark
my hard desire
hard
does endure
this dune
        from where
the poem
        a
        spume
   in distress
ex
  pl
    odes

        𝄞

today the circus is in town
everyone called me too
i find everything brings me down
these days of stuffing sausage
between triumph and waterloo

        ●

you
whom we call
when love's all
when we're scared
and grieving
when we're thirsty
and water's lacking
you
only you
whom we follow
until it's finally
in check
or in flames
any sound
any at all
can be your voice
your zoom-zoom-humming
frightful edge
in the shape
of a sudden hedge
loosened pebble
deviled sky
could be your shade
or your homecoming

ॐ

frustrating waits
eves of sweet dates
raw materials
with so many stars
what are your rates?

shaman's prayer

may i be bolt weeds
in my friends' hearts
a tree force
at the edge of the creek
stone in the fountain
stars
   on the border
      of the abyss

windmill of verses
moved by the breeze
in bohemian nights

a day will come
when whatever i say
will be poetry

to-day
give me
the wisdom of caetano
never to read the news
the madness of glauber
ever to sever an extra head to lose
the fury of décio
never to obey a normal-verse muse

to see
is painful
to hear
is painful
to have
is painful
to lose
is painful

but to feel pain
is a painless sensation
delightful
experimentation

remember me
as someone who would
listen to the raindrops
as if attending mass
hesitating, mixing class,
hasty steps or lazy stops

i bore the white wall
so the moon can come in
to verify with the one,
that loose in my dreams,
is larger than the night

like a stump dear to the dump
incredulous james
i touch the sores
that i've amassed
from the mutilated
past

i touch the void
that void that will not stop
that nothingness now
that had
my face
in place

no-no negation
for no nothing
declares such damnation

so much wonder
would marvel to last
here down under
where nothing will last
where nothing ceases
to be a venture so vast

yes
i opted for a prose
this goddess
spews only silly stew
talks about things
as if new

i didn't want prose
only the idea
an idea of prose
a troubador rose
blissful semen
slippery slime

a poetry of pores

were it not this and it would be less
were it not so much and it would be almost

poem on the page
bite of a child
into ripe fruit

paralyzing gaze n.91

the cobra's gaze lies
                belays
                paralyzes the bird

            my gaze
            falls from me
            lunar
            laser

my awakening   awakening
my desperate love   of my gaze
my evil eye   alarming

        my gaze
        reader

who eats your work like i eat this slice or take this sip?

erase myself
dilute myself
disarm myself
until later
after me
after us
after all
nothing is left
but charm

heart
THIS SIDE UP
written below
FRAGILE

may everything pass

may the night pass
may the plague pass
may the summer pass
may the winter pass
may the wars pass
and may peace pass

may what is born pass
may what not even pass
may what it does pass
may what makes it up pass

may everything pass
and may it pass very well

blowing on this bamboo
i only take away
what the wind's given it

coffin for a drawer

this is the drawer of vice
rimbaud had one
hendrix many
mallarmé had none

this is the drawer
of an impossible cabinet

poetry he used to make

and most their leave would take
such was the poetry he'd make

poetry he used to make

and the poetry he'd make
was not the type
to put our souls at stake

poetry he used to make

and the poetry he'd make
another philosophical wake

poetry he used to make

and the poetry he'd make
was done for family's sake

poetry he used to make

and its halt
caused our party to break

so much poetry he'd make
poetry will one day stay awake

exit and reversal

inside
it's just rehearsal

❧

saw no refrain
saw well again

saw here
saw beyond
saw not the train

saw no refrain
saw it all
not life's vein

saw all there was
not seeing life
all that life does

PSYCHEDELIC CURVE
the mind jumps the tracks beneath

ARISTOTELIC LOGIC
to my children i shan't bequeath

perfume
evaporates
for the fire
up there
the high fire
expires
perfumes
you
launch
summit
summoned
mist
fireflies

headline

WHEN A POET TAKES THE SHOT
THE GOALIE WORRIES NOT

i wanted so much
to be a poet of damnation
the masses suffering
while i'm in deep meditation

i wanted so much
to be a social poet
my face all burnt
by the breath of crowds

instead
look at me here
adding salt
to this thin soup
barely enough for two

the machine
gulps down pages
spits out poems
gulps down pages
spits out some ads

UPPERCASE
lowercase

the machine
gulps down carbon
spits out copy
spits out copy
gulps down poets
spits out prose

LOWERCASE
uppercase

night
drips a star in my eye
and passes by

i'm tired of phrases polished
by pale-faced angels
palm trees clapping
as parades pass
now i want the pelting
rain of petrous palaver
passing out beatings

i awaken   soon i sleep
i sleep   soon i awaken
neither   memories   nor diaries
with my own self i debate
from here til   there
from there til   later

i've been a thing
written on a slate
my muse being lost
now just my name
on a blouse so embossed

the master spins the globe
shakes his head and says, louder

the world is like this and that

books students school-gear
disappear through the windows

clouds of white chalk powder

in the class struggle
all arms are good ones
stones
nights
poems

[originally written in Spanish]

you stop
so as to see
what awaits you

only a cloud
separates you
from the stars

i won't argue
for destiny's fine

whatever it brings
i'll just sign

❦

the sun writes
on your skin
the name of another race

yet disdains
in each grape
the history of the sky
of the winds
and the rains

๛

life is the cows
that you put in the river
to attract the piranhas
while the herd gets across

●

you are
with whom i speak
and do not sprick

centaur

man-horse

you
do not exist

i must create you of course

❡

check this mire

everything that respires
conspires

●

ana sees alice
as if seeing an empty chalice
as if nowhere were the palace
as if ana did not even exist

seeing ana
alice discovers analysis
ana avails herself of
alice's analysis
and makes herself Ana Alice

❡

life can surely vary
what had less value
begins to have more
when it goes crazy

a wind
that is a wind
will stay

a wall
a wall
won't wait

my rhythm
beats in the wind
and dis
    in
      te
        gra
          tes

johnny? do you hear me? yes yes of course your mother
and i forgive you we've already forgiven you i said we
forgive you it can happen of course it can happen to
anyone i said to anyone sure to anyone do you hear me
yes we forgive you i said your mother your mother
forgives you yes you do you hear me now whatever it is
of course all forgiven your mother forgives mothers
always forgive everything i said everything forgives yes
your mother and i we never never fathers always forgive
i forgive you forgive you forgive you now go to sleep
my poor johnny sleep i said i've already said that i
forgive you your mother forgives you now johnny do
you hear johnny do you hear when i say do you hear me
yes johnny do you do you do

[partially written in English]

[87]

laughter for gil

your laughter is
reflected in your singing
perfect rhyme
sunshine
on a golden tooth

"everything is gonna be alright"

your laughter
says yes
your laughter is
satisfying

while the sun
that mimics your laughter
doesn't come out

❦

so far away i said see you soon
a bit of everything happened once again
and it was once all made of games
that other time that knew not how to be
because it came back and back and back
without knowing that one of the two
will never be three

❦

i want the victory
of the underdog team

valiant

coward

the champion
left for dead

5 to nothing

on its own home field

circus
inside
the bread

a little of mao
in every poem that teaches

the smaller the size the more
like how far china reaches

all of a sudden
i recall the green
of the color green
the greenest ever seen
the happiest color
the saddest color
the green you wear now
the green you were wearing
the day i've first seen you
the day you've seen me too

all of a sudden
i sold my children
to an american family
they've got the cars
they've got the money
they've got the houses
the lawns are so funny
only this way they can come back
and enjoy copacabana when it's sunny

words and music; recorded as "Verdura" by Caetano Veloso,
1979

letter to random chance

one card in the deck
  a large razor
can cut without noise
  the eye of the jack
the king at sword's edge
  water flour poise
just one pass of the sword
  toward the queen's neck

if i knew things were like this
i wouldn't have been born
and never would have known

nobody is born knowing it all
it even looks like i'm a bit forgetful
but this is something i always recall

white clouds
pass by
    in clouds of white

my friends
when they take my hand
they always leave
something else
presence
gaze
warmthremembrance

my friends
whenever we band
they leave their hands
in mine

pauloleminski
is a mad dog
who must be slain
burned stoned beaten
dead with a stick
sink him or else
the son of a bitch
might make it rain
all over our picnic

burn me a kiss   bonfire of remnants of love
burn   if you can
burn the suspicion   that in my breast must turn
break my day   that in so many stones explodes
burn my name   that in your flame may transform
this tempest   this life in times of poetry
burn me so much   that i shall always keep in mind
the wind advancing me   forward all winds left behind

twelfth night has gone by
the year advances to may
the kings have moved on
flower
mary
labor
the people stayed on
mother
majority
the peoples stayed on

&

we were born in diverse poems
destiny wished us to find each other
in the same strophe sister and brother
in the same verse the same phrases

rhyme at first sight we saw one another
exchanging what was synonymous
our gazes no longer anonymous

having read this far along
the same tracks and lines
of mine of yours of ours blended

●

i woke up flat
all was sharp and tense

the sun was there
it just didn't make sense

Love, then,
also, ends?
Not as far as I know.
What I know
is that it turns
into raw material
that life
takes charge of
turning into strife.
Or into rhyme ethereal.

i parisize
i newyorkize
i moscovitate
without leaving the bar

i just don't get up and go
because there are countries
that i can't even madagascar

telescopic sight
of a precision rifle
or a broken window
where a child in convolution
can see the things that are
scenes from the russian revolution?

plum leaves
love 'em
or leave 'em

stop
i confess
i'm a poet

each day that breaks
a rose is risen
on my face

stop
i confess
i'm a poet

only my love is my god

i am its prophet

WHAT IF IT
WERE REAL
THIS ENHANCEMENT
GIL SAW IN GIL
AS THE VOYAGE
VIA GIL?

clay takes
whatever form
that you may want

you don't even know
that you're just doing
what the clay wants you to

great angle for the zap agency

the cities of the west
on the plains
at the seashore
next to rivers
beasts shot down
during the night

during the day
a motor keeps them all
alive and lit up   PROFIT

at night
ghosts of things not said
shadows of things not done
come
on tiptoes
to mess with your dreams

the cities of the west
scream
scream
crazy demons
all night long until dawn

the poem
on the page
the drapes

at the window
a murderous
landscape

rise apogee and fall of the life passion and death
of the poet as a being who cries while
it rains outside and someone sings
the last hope to arrive
at the station of light and catch the first train
to far beyond the bluish mountains on the horizon
that separates him from the dawn of his life

winter
spring
a poet is one
who feels it ring

i never wanted to be
the distinguished customer
asking for this and that
red wine
thank you
hasta la vista

i wanted to intrude
with both feet
on the doorman's chest
saying to the mirror
- just shut up
and to the clock
- down with your hands

to the purity dreamed of by
the popular songwriter

one day being able to write
a lullaby

&

it's only life
but i like it

let's go
baby
    let's go

this is life

it is not
        rock and roll

[originally written in English]

[98]

ideolacrimation

in what i may feel
yes a bit of paper
a whole reel of tape
and a great deal of ink

i grab this world
hit it on my head
memory may go dead
maybe it finally

haiku of the world
haiku of me

water that knows me
in me it flows
the flame of my throes

two leaves in the sandals

autumn also
wants to walk

tonight
even the stars
smell like orange blossoms

the palm tree trembles
clap your hands for the tree
its merit resembles

the watch on its last
the ears hear
 tick-tacks from the past

pity
  pity
    the bird

to
 the
  city

[originally written in English]

the shooting star
fell to me still a char
 in the palm of my hand

night
 the wasp stings
   the evening star

with each jolt
does come and go
a revolt

knock where you dare
you can be sure
 there's someone there

it's high up here

been years i don't hear
frogs' crying choir

green the fallen tree
turns yellow
the last time it can be

nothing turns me off
i'm still going to father
the brothers karamazov

by a thread
        the thread fled
                the dreaded scythe

in the mirror
        sideways glance
the color of dreams
        of yesterday

humming
bird
in the rain

no
drop
will detain

in the street
   without resisting

people call me

i go back to existing

    autumn moon
so much sleepless swoon
   because of you

this fact won't change
no matter what i state

that leaf of lettuce
is the last on the plate

leaning over a hole
viewing the void
     come and go

watchdog behind home's rail
my guardian angel
    wags its tail

on the floor
my sandals

footprints in patches

any way to catch them?

a technicolor bird
by the fruit-colored twilight
 pilfers the flower

a miracle of winter
now the water
 in oranges is gold

xavante
so many xxxxx
 avanti

a luxury to know

beyond these roof tiles
a sky of stars

it won't rain long
may all the ox tongues
 grow ever more strong

jealousy
just dies

flying on
    empty
      the fire
        flies

times are dark

a rain full of stars
leaves on the paper
these letters' mark

i laugh
  at what i don't laugh at
        laughing
           at the children laughing

  to warm up at a bonfire
the cold i feel
  when contemplating stars?

  my hair falling out
with each strand
  a thousand years of haiku

with so many leaves
autumn
perceives not how many

❀

first day of class
in the classroom
 me and the room

ॐ

clothes to raise on the line

may god be awash in praise
among a fine wash

❀

rain comes from above

they run off as if it
were coming from behind

❀

let the indian flute
always say

not yet

❀

through
the magnolia
white

the
mourning
blue
red light
in sight

sol-te

sol-te

sol = sun

te = thee

sol-te = sun-thee, sun thyself

solte = singular imperative of the verb *soltar*, to loosen, unfasten, untie, let loose, let go, free, relax, slacken, relinquish, release

SOLTE O SOL

LET THE SUN GO

SOLTE
TODO SOL
TODA SORTE

PODE
QUE VOLTE

RELEASE
EVERY SUN
EVERY SORT

THEY MAY
COME BACK

light time
of the verb to go

no one light
at any time

to go being
as the verb goes
nary a care
while wanting

not *every* year
is a work
not every work
is *masterful*
some are maternal
others sororal
some

     atmosphere

distaste
for pleasure
i try

disknowledge
of passing
on the fly

certainty
fortune
here
i
lie

me
so isosceles
you
an angle
hypotheses
about my
erotic art

theses
syntheses
antitheses
mind where
you step
it might be
my heart

SUN
MOON
WHY JUST ONE OF EACH
AT A TIME
                    IN THE SKY
                  FLOATING BY

you used to love me
tweets
the daisy so rife

though the daisy
is sweet
it bitters this life

SIGN
I ASSIGN
AT NIGHT
THE DOOM

TO BE
WHAT
THE SHADE
DESIRED
AS A GROOM

TILL EVEN HER ALL

ON FOOT
IN PETALS
FROM PETAL
TO PETAL

TILL SHE'S
    UN-PETAL-E D

by ear

di   vi
ded   out
'tween
the
gaze
&
the
glaze
i hear doubt

all

that

i've

read

irritates

me

when

i hear

rita

lee

hai-cry for Bashō

NO   FA
  OR MO THER

        IN   SIGH S
                    T

PERHAPPINESS

[originally written in English]

if
not
for
land

then
trans
for
nation

suddenly
all comes
u n g l u e d

i don't do
i explude

the impression of your
body on mine
set me in *motion*

from the tree
the A
    a U
      a T
       a U
        a M
         a N

a   lone
   tumble

by all indications

all things indicate

r j x s p l u f s
s u p g r u j
Q S r g e k o
t z j k o r
u t r
u s

to see the end you'll have to wait

WHY THE SAD FACE
TWICE?

IN LIFE

NO ONE PAYS HALF PRICE.

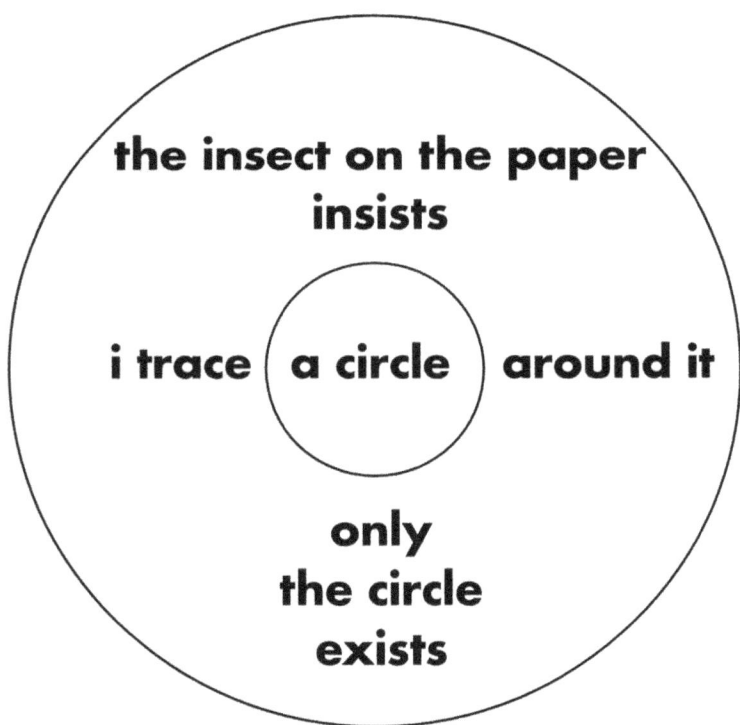

the insect on the paper
insists

i trace (a circle) around it

only
the circle
exists

from sound to sound

i show silence around

to be like a sibyl

from gong to gong

the silence to sound

i show along

i made thee
now

i am thy god
oh poem

take a bow
and a knee
to adore
me

SYL   LA   BLE

MY BEND

W   O   R   D   S

WITHOUT

E   N   D

E   N   D

E   N   D

KAMI QUASE

hint at it
graffiti
is the limit

sweetie:
graffiti
ends the entreaty

LUA NA AGUA
LUA NA AGUA

ALGUMA LUA
A UL A

LUA ALGUMA
A UL A

moon on water <moon on water>

some moon <water>

any moon <moon>

semiotic stories

papajoyceatwork

(Night. Joyce begins to write)
Madmanam eye! Light gone out!
(Falls over the sheet)
Mustmakesomething! Reverythming!
(Bites his lips and laughs out loud)
A poorirish is a writer mehrlichtsearching, yesternighteternities!
(It thunders. Lightnings brighten up the room. Joyce goes on)
Thomasmorrows? Horriver!
Nice and sweet – the speech of England, damnyou! Dont?
Must destroy it, just like a destroyer would do it yourself!
                              Like a vermin. Yes, I no.
Done to Ireland! What have they done? It will do.
Beforeblacksblanco, we are even, this very evening! Think is so.
My vengeance will be as big as say a country as big as say Brazil.
Someday my prince will come. Our prince: Seabastião!
Arrise, Lewisrockandcarrol!
Waterrestrela, am I a dayer?
Just a wakewriter.

[originally written mostly in English]

the assassin was the scribe

My professor of syntactical analysis was the type of
nonexistent subject.
A pleonasm, the main predicate of his life,
common as a paradigm of the first conjugation.
Between a subordinant clause and an adverbial
adjunct he had no doubts: he always found an asyndetic
way to torture us with an appositive.
He married grammatical rectitude.
He was unhappy.
Possessive like a pronoun.
And she was bitransitive.
He tried to go to the USA.
It didn't work out.
They discovered an indefinite article in his suitcase.
His moustache's exclamation point declined expletives,
connectives and passive agents, the entire time.
One day I killed him with a direct object straight to the head.

inventions

hai-ku: hi-fi

I.
it's raining
on the only one
that remained

a horse like rattled elf
i follow with my eyes
to horse myself

in spans of fright
spontaneous oh
spantaneous

the
crow
w
row
is
neg
a
c
ti
v
e

the
boa
cons
str
ict
or
e
ea
eat
s
an
ox

the
cat
is
as
s
low
as
re
read
d
ding
g

the
vac
c
cuum
is
wher
e
the
c
cows
go
to
d
dr
ink

the
rain
a
in
is
bi
big
g
ger
th
an
an
the
ra
in
co
at

and
th
is
ve
ry
sa
me
me
mo
mon
onth
on
th
that
at
the
sa
me
ta
ble

the stern warning of the bronze gates
of the manor mansions
the warning of the gates of the mansions
the warning of the gates
the warning
the anxiety

❧

materismophos

temasirsphomo

thermospasmio

trimesphosoma

metrophasimos

morstimesapho

amorphostemis

ismarotemosph

israomosphite

phitomormeosa

mesamorphitos

iphastormesom

maephortossim

saotesmorphem

phaseortomims

motormephasis

matermophisos

metamorphosis

PARKER
TEXACO
                    ESSO
                    FORD   ADAMS
                              FABER
MELHORAL
SONRISAL
                         RINSO
                         LEVER
                         GESSY
RCE
GE
                         MOBILOIL
                         KOLYNOS

          ELECTRIC
          COLGATE
          MOTORS
                         GENERAL

casas pernambucanas

○: estão perto.
Mais dois corredores, me pegam (continuo correndo).
Passo pela porta, o sinal●.
Atravesso o labirinto de ◐,◖,◑,◕,◙,○,◒,●,◕,◕, em
direção a um ponto ⊕ - encruzilhada versus encruzilhadas.
Fecho a porta.
Chego ao beco sem saída: ◑. Correndo, ouço seus gritos de triunfo.
◒,●,◙,◕,◕,◑,⊕,◐,◒,◐,◙: corredores.
Agora, os ◒,◕,◐,○,◒,◑,◐ e os ◙ estão nos meus
calcanhares.
Infinitos.
Grandes.
Ferozes.
Me tranco no último corredor: fim da linha.
Batem na porta.
Tomo a pílula que me transporta para outra dimensão. Um segundo,
já sinto os efeitos.
Outro lugar. Sou outro.
A cabeça roda, rodopia, me transformo em flor, no planeta Vênus.
- Não está aqui, escapou - diz
Meus perseguidores tomam suas pílulas, vêm atrás de mim.
Tomo outra pílula, me transformo em pedra: planeta Saturno.
◑,◕,◕,◒, vêm atrás.
Tomo outra. Sou sombra no Sol.● , ◕, vêm atrás. Outra. Vapor em
Júpiter.
Outra. Eles - atrás. Outra.
Sou idéia na cabeça de um homem do planeta Terra.
Qual o homem, qual a idéia?
Continuo correndo, fugindo.
Chego, finalmente, à conclusão:
Ninguém vai me alcançar agora que ●

O: they are close.

Two more runners, they catch me (I keep running).

I walk through the door, the sign .

I cross the labyrinth of , , , , , , , , , , toward a point - crossroad versus crossroads.

I close the door.

I reach the dead end: . Running, I hear their triumphant shouts.

   , , , , , , , , , : runners.

Now, the , , , , , , and the are on my heels.

Infinite.

Large.

Fierce.

I lock myself in the last corridor: end of the line.

They knock on the door.

I take the pill that transports me to another dimension. One second, I already feel the effects.

Another place. I'm someone else.

The head swirls, twirls, I turn into a flower, on planet Venus.

"He's not here, he's escaped."

My persecutors take their pills, they come after me.

I take another pill, turn myself to stone: planet Saturn.

   , , , , come up behind.

I take another pill. I'm a shadow in the Sun. , , up behind. Another pill. Steam on Jupiter.

Another pill. Them - behind. Another pill.

I am an idea in the head of a man on planet Earth.

Which man, what's the idea?

I keep running, running away.

I finally come to the conclusion:

No one will catch up with me now that

III. distracted we shall overcome

[1987]

Toward Alice,
accomplice in this crime of lese-life
called poetry.
To Antonio Cícero, Arnaldo "Titã" Antunes,
and – especially – to Itamar Assumpção.

What arrow is that on the heel of that there? To judge by the feather, it is Persian, by the precision of the shot, a master. Now, the Persian masters are always old. And master, Persian and old, it can only be Artaxerxes or a brother, or a friend, or a disciple, or else simply someone who was passing by and took a crazy shot in a lazy moment of distraction.

Catatau, p. 33.

distracted we shall overcome

notice to the shipwrecked

This page, for example,
wasn't born to be read.
  It was born to be pallid,
merely to plagiarize the Iliad,
  something keeping quiet
a leaf that returns to the branch,
  long after it was felled.

  It was born to be sand,
who knows Andromeda, Antarctica,
  Himalaya, a syllable felt,
it was born to be the last one
  the one not yet born.

  Words brought from afar
by the waters of the Nile,
  one day, this page, papyrus,
will have to be transcribed,
  into symbols, into Sanskrit,
into all the dialects of India,
  it will have to say good day,
to what is only told in whispers,
  it will have to be the harsh stone
where someone dropped the glass.
  Isn't that the way life is?

☙

the law of how

   There ought to be again
a breeze that attains
   some features of rain
for the last snow white.

   Until then, please observe
the strictest of disciplines.
   Maximal shadows might
derive from minimal light

                ꙮ

minifesto

   hail the rage of this night
the hefty splinter sudden fury
   crazy beast cow let loose
red-haired light against the day
   so much & so late you've awoken

   may the calm of this afternoon
simply perish in gold
   at last, more silk
this death, this fraud,
   when prosperous

   may it live and die above all
this day, vile metal,
   deaf, dumb and blind,
in it was all and, if being were all,
   i can't know everything
even if springtime will know
   or if one day i'll know that
neither my knowing nor being just so

I did come the hard way,
the line that never ends,
　　the line that strikes a stone,
the word breaks down a corner,
　　minimal empty line,
the line, an entire life,
　　word, word of mine.

●

adminimystery

　　When the mystery arrives,
it will find me fast asleep,
　　half on saturday time,
half, oh sunday be mine.
　　Neither silence nor sound ought exist,
as the mystery expands a great deal.
　　Silence so surely is senseless,
I simply can't help but observe.
　　Yes mystery is something, I feel,
more time, and less place.
　　When the mystery returns,
may my sleep be so free,
　　that no scares still exist
that may keep me on my feet.

　　Midnight, open book.
Moths and mosquitoes look
　　to land on uncertain text.
Could it be the blank on the leaf,
　　or light that looks like an object?
Perhaps the smell of black and ink,
　　that acts there as some remnant?
Or could insects have discovered
　　their kinship intersected
with the letters of the alphabet?

minimal distances

  a text of bat calls
is guided by echoes
  a text text of blindness
an an an ancient anti-echo
  a scream on tall walls all wall
beams back green gleam cream
  with me with your wherewithal
to hear is to see if to see
  or if if me then to follow thee?

●

oh how we miss amnesia

to a friend who lost his memory

  Memory is a recent thing.
Just yesterday, who could remember?
  Did the thing come before,
or, rather, was it wordish lore?
  The loss of remembrance,
not such a big deal.
  Clouds stay white for real.
Seas as green as they ever were.

●

iceberg

An Arctic ballad,
I'd, of course, like to entice.
A practice so pallid,
three verse-lines of ice.
A phrase of the surface
where a life-phrase never
could be possible.
Phrase, no. None whatsoever.
Null and lyrical,
reduced to purely minimal,
a blinking of the spiritual,
a lone unique unit.
Yet I speak. And my speaking is
provoking equivocating clouds
(or hives of monologues?).
Yes, winter, we are alive.

●

by a refraction of a second

all in me
full speed ahead
all in this way
all by a thread
all so as if
all were in heat
all gingerly tread
all just psst

everything around me
left in a sprawl
as if things
were all
after all

Surfing well on every wave
belongs to the Heavenly Father,
    rounding moons to make them brave
or making me be born, a Paraná-er.
    We, the people, were only given
this damned ability to give in
    and turn love into naught.

may the expression pass

    Those artifacts
that might express my anguish,
    some of them come easy-ish,
while many actually cost me.
    Sometimes it's a shard of glass,
months turned into shouts,
    other times I have no doubts,
some days, yes, I do believe.
    Then we'll all be geniuses
when the privies of the world
    vomit back
all the toilet tissue.

the minimum of the maximum

   Slow time,
rapid space,
  the more I think,
the less I trace.
  If I don't get this
that passes me inside,
  does it really matter?
I kidnap rhythm.
  An avid spacetime,
slow insidespace,
  and when I approach,
  only the minimum
in terms of maximum.

＊

ascendant sign

  May every mirror not
reflect this hieroglyph.
  Nor every eye
decipher this ideogram of.
  If everything exists
to end up in a book,
  if all enigmatizes
the souls who can love!

**beyond soul
(a gram later)**

   There my heart from far away
to make a return is aspiring.
   My chest is wrought bronze to say:
NO VACANCY NOT HIRING.
   What use for me is this fine thing
that will not stop its beating?
   Seems much more like a timepiece
that's just gone mad repeating.
   Why would I need one who weeps,
when this way I chose is best,
   and the void that outside seeps
falls smoothly on my breast?

●

full pause

   A place where's done
what's already been done,
   the blank of the page,
sum of all texts,
   time departed
when, in writing,
   an exempt leaf
was needed.

   No page
was ever clean.
   Even the most Saharian,
Arctic one, signifies.
   That there never was,
a blank page.
   In the depths, they all shout,
pallid from so much.

●

shit and gold

Shit is poison on tap.
Nothing, nevertheless,
is more beautiful
than a simple lovely crap.
The rich shit, shit do the poor,
kings shit and fairies all the more.
No feces will ever come close
to the shit of the one you love most.

the pair that appears to me

The language I didn't create,
does weigh inside my fears,
 tongue that doesn't terminate,
it's made of ouches and heres.
 'Twas such a beautiful language,
music, more than words,
 of Hittite, there's some angles
of Java's beach, two-thirds.
 A perfect linguistic vase,
it had almost no objects.
 Pronouns of the right case
never ended up as subjects.
 Everything was multiplied,
tripled verbs, long-winded rash.
 Screams alone were rescinded.
The rest went to the trash.
 Two leos in each rubble,
two jumps in each hop,
 I who saw only the half,
silence, everything double.

the art of tea

  just yesterday
i asked a friend to tea
  to stay silently
there with me

  and come he did
kind of randomly to sit
  practically said nothing
and that was really it

                    ●

proem

  There's no verse,
everything's prose,
  strides of light
in a mirror,
  verse, illusion
of optics,
  green,
the red light.

  Something
made of breezes,
  of sorrow
and of calm,
  inside
such a poem,
  what poetry
would so pose?

                    ●

Today, I woke up earlier
and, blue, did I realize.
  There's really only one secret.
Everything's before your eyes.

unencontraries

  I told the word to rhyme,
but it did not obey.
  It spoke of skies, a bay, a rose
in Greek, in silence, in prose.
  Seemed out of its wits,
the silent syllable.

  I told the phrase to dream,
in a labyrinth it was inspired.
  Making poetry, I feel, only this.
Having an army sent
    to conquer an extinct empire.

What's meant to be said

to Haroldo de Campos,
translator maximus

What's meant to be said will say.
Don't go doing
  what I, one day, always did.
Don't just keep meaning and wanting,
  something I wanted in no way.
What's meant to be said will say.
  Only by saying in another
  what, one day, was said
will you, one day, happily stay.

●

a meter of shouts
(liquid machines)

Read indexes,
a thousand lynx eyes,
  within my filmic guise,
leonardos da vinci.
  Open oh you arks, archives,
hives of equivocation,
  closed down,
what purpose can books have?

Books made of glass,
discs, high key, low key,
  things I sell by the meter,
they buy from me by the kilo.
  Liquid blades, laminate
parallel lines,
  how much will they give me
for my own ideas?

●

lucky at games
unlucky in love
  what good does
luck in love do for me
  if love is a gamble and
gambling's not my forté,
  my love?

clear keeping quiet about a city without ruins (ruingrams)

In Brasilia, I admired.
Not the Niemeyer law,
  people's lives
penetrating the schemes
  like blood paint
in the blotter,
  growing the peopled red,
between stone and stone,
  on and into the earth.

In Brasilia, I admired.
The small clandestine restaurant,
  criminal for being
outside the permitted quarter.
  Yes, Brasilia.
I admired the time
  that has covered with years
your impeccable math.

Goodbye, City.
The trespass, of course, not the law.
  Greatly you've admired me,
I've greatly admired you.

I carry the weight of moons,
Three passions gone bad and sour,
   A sahara of paginated dunes,
These infinite after-hours.

   Living at night
Made me lord of the fire.
   To you, I leave slumber.
Not the dreams.
   I myself shall carry those.

                    ⋎

a few fewer names

   Name plus name equal to name,
some names less, some names more.
   Less is more or less,
not all the names are the same.

   One thing is the thing, even or odd,
another is the name, even and even,
   portrait of a thing when oddly clean,
thing that things leave upon passing.

   Name of an animal, a month, or a star,
names of my loves, animal names,
   the sum of all names,
will never give a thing, no frames.

   Cities pass. Only names will stay.
What thing's painful inside the name
   that's nameless yet telling
not a thing that you say?

                    ●

return left open

   Ambiguous returns
around ambiguous departures,
   how many ambiguities
to commit as life turns?
   He who leaves appears to be
one who's left the soul cracked.
   Who knocks more on the door?
One who departs or one who comes back?

●

re: naucitals of nautical wrecks

   the letter A s
inks in the A
   tlantic
and pacific i com
   template the struggle
between the rapid letter
   and the slow
ocean

   thus do i
found myself and flounder
among all the shipwrecked
naucital
   of the most profound
nautical
   wreck

●

deep down

at bottom, at bottom,
deep down at the bottom,
us folks would like
to see our problems
resolved by decree

from this day forward,
that grief with no relief
will be considered null and void
and about it — perpetual silence

extinguished by law all remorse,
damned be those who may look back,
back there behind nothing is left,
and nothing else

but problems are not solved,
problems have big families,
on sundays they all go out for a walk
the problem, his wife
and other small little problems

*

sans buddhism

   A poem that is good
ends up nil-nil.
   It ends up with.
Not the way I would.
   It begins without.
With, let's say, a certain line,
   poisonous letter,
bolero. Or less.
   Takes some out here, puts some away,
in a place, not a way.
   Moves on from itself.
Safe and sorry, dead of old age,
   alone on the stage.

●

   love, in such a rush,
a moment ago it seemed too much,
   and now it's just a hush

   oh, craziness in bunches,
hearts exchanging roses,
   and punches

the unseen guest

I left someone in this hall
who was really quite distinguished
   from someone no one would call,
when I would be extinguished.
   Resembling me on a leash,
but only on a surface, blurred.
   Deep down inside, I, a word,
was nothing but pastiche.
   A remnant, a trace, a day,
my uncles, my mothers, my parents
   should they call me back inside,
I may still just go astray.
   But there, right there, in that space,
example of me never ceases,
   something, someone, a thousand pieces,
half beginning, half and half, endless chase.

·

steel in bloom

> *for Koji Sakaguchi,*
> *friendly portal between*
> *Japan and Brazil*

One who has never seen
that flower, knife and fierce beast
   have done forever and whatever,
and the flower force the knife forces
   on the frail flesh,
a little less, a little more,
   one who has never seen
the tenderness at the fore
   on the edge of the samurai blade,
this one will never be able to aid.

·

the moon at the movies

The moon went to the picture show,
they played a funny movie,
  the story of a starlet
with no boyfriend, with no beau.

She didn't have the usual flame
for she was just a little star,
  who, losing shine, remains a char,
and no one says that's such a shame!

She was such a lonely star,
at her no one would look,
  and all the light she had and took
would fit inside a single jar.

So full of sadness was the moon
with that story of love that was missed
  that to this day she still insists:
"May dawn come now, please real soon!"

●

anch'io son pittore

  fra angelico
all the while he painted
  a madonna and child
would kneel and pray
  as if he were a boy

  before the work he prayed
as if it were a sin
  to paint that holy lady
without kneeling on his shins

  he prayed as if the work
were of god and not of a man

                ●

  go ahead and keep reality
that downer of a place where
  down the drain everything goes

  me i want to live in actuality
with those american picture shows

lithograph

A statue's hand.
Temple. Column. Arch of triumph.
Twelve fifty.
Any and all stones in Europe
are suspected of being
more than they planned.

Blessed are the stones of my land
for they were never anything but stones.
The moon cools them down
and the sun warms them up.

●

trending rhymes

1930	1960	1980
love	man	loves
dove	can	shoves
	wan	

yesterday I had the impression
that God tried to talk to me
I didn't lend him my ears

who am I to talk to Sir Divine?
let him take care of his business
I'll take care of mine

●

186,000 miles per second

What music do
mosquitoes like?
Schubert, Wagner,
Debussy?
They like nothing,
judging by this fellow here.
Just a solo of silence,
yes, indeed,
is what I hear.

cardiac arrest

This dryness of mine
this sentimental lack
that no one can hold back
it comes from down my spine

It surges from a zone sans glow
at the source of what I feel
I'm so very sorry
that feeling is so slow

as if i were julio plaza

pleasure
of pure perception
  may the senses be
the critique
  of reason

lucks and cuts

the clear line   scissors trace   on the blank leaf

separates   the leaf from the form   the form

a devil inhabits the whites of the eye of the page

clear   occult   among   the clarities

the void passes   and leaves a longing

●

imprecise premise

(how many Curitibas fit in a lone Curitiba?)

Small cities,
oh, how painful is this silence,
chants, litanies,
all I don't even ponder,
this excess
that makes me see all senses,
imprecise premise,
definitive sloth
about what rises, indecisive,
the more or less of incense.
Village of Our Lady
of the Light of the Pines,
have mercy on us.

❦

hard feelings

(a riddle for Martha)

Oceans,
emotions,
ships, ships,
and other relationships,
keep us going
through the fog
and wandering mist.

What is it
that I missed?

[Originally written in English]

❦

indirect subject

I wish I could find a way
to make everything perfect,
for the thing to be the project,
everything born so satisfied to stay.
I wish to see the other side,
the over there, the middle side,
where triangles are square
and crooked ones seem fair.
I wish I had an angle right.
I'm so fed up to have to see
I know not when I've lost the fight,
of being the indirect subject of me.

for leda to read me
silk tissue is needed
stone and sand are needed
for it to read me leda

it needs legend and clarity
it needs being and a siren
just for it to see me

pity it should be leda
whoever you are who reads me

[This poem has been set to music twice. Once by Moraes Moreira,
another by Itamar Assumpção. Would you like to try?]

seem and disappear

It seems like it was yesterday.
Everything seemed to be something.
  Day seemed to be night.
And wine seemed to be roses.
  It even seems to be a lie,
everything seemed to be something.
  Time seemed to be short,
and we seemed so much alike.
  The pain, above all,
seemed to be pleasure.
  Seeming was everything
things knew how to do.
  Thy neighbor, myself.
So easy to be similar,
  when I had a mirror
to serve as an example.
  But vice versa and look at life.
Nothing resembles anything.
  The tape doesn't match
the tragedy on stage.
  It seems like it was yesterday.
The rest, may things themselves
  be free to say.

ore or less

ore or less

(prayer for disbelief)

Lord,
I ask for powers over slumber,
  this sun in which I set myself
to suffer my ore or less,
  shadows, maybe dreams of an elf.
  I want strength for the leap
from the abyss where I'm deep
  into the hiatus where I'm missing.
  Well inside me, the stone,
and at the feet of the stone,
  this shadow, stone fading alone.
  Stone, letter, star on the loose,
I want to live with no faith at all,
  to lead a life that will be missed
without ever knowing who it is.

volatile

Walking years around outback,
I never saw a dead bird once,
  as I saw a bird be born in fact.

Just where do these flights end?
Dissolved in thin air, in breezes, in the act?
  Are they soluble in water or in wine?

Who knows, some infernal eye disease.
Or are these little birds eternal?

how can it be?

It's sounding strange, this morning,
all that was always mine, how can it be?
    How can it be that that sound out there,
the sounds of life, the voice of every day,
    seem like science fiction?

    How can it be that this word,
that I've seen and said a thousand times,
    now means nothing at all,
unless the day, the night, the dawn,
    unless everything is nothing of that sort?

    Perhaps I'm no longer the same.
May the light, may it be, may the sky and so much.
    May everything that can so be.
It just can't be that much.

                    ⁘

    Marginal is he who writes on the edge,
leaving the pages blank
    for the landscape to pass
to clear everything with its passage.

    Marginal, writing in-between the lines,
forever with unknowing stricken
    which came first,
the egg or the chicken.

                    ✱

rosa rilke raimundo correia

An eyelid,
one more, another and others,
   eventually dozens
of eyelids over eyelids
   trying to make
of my darkness
   something other
than teardrops

three halves

Midday,
a day and a half,
half day, half night,
half of this poem
won't appear in the photo,
a half, half is gone.

But then the third half,
the one less a dose
of mathematical truth
than punches, shots, or kicking,
comes and goes as something
of or, of neither, even almost.

As if we all possessed
halves that don't match,
three parts, unstormy weather,
three times or times three,
as if almost, existing,
we only missed the whether.

impure spirit
rare breath afire
  the air trying here
architect
  and vague flight
        vampire

woe unto them
sharing love without a fight
  those who allowed
a brand-new hurt
  to become an old blight

woe to those who have loved one another
not knowing that love is a homemade thing
  and that stones only don't fly
because they don't even want to
  not because they have no wings

the punctual delay

  Yesterdays todays, loves and hate,
any good to check the clock?
  Nothing could be otherwise,
except when it was logical.
  No one ever made a late arrival.
Blessings and misfortunes
  always there without a rival.
Everything else is plagiarism.
  Is this encounter
of time and space by chance
  more than my dream in a trance
or just one more poetic stance

Not everything grows old.
The purple glow
  under pure water,
ah, if I only could.

  Not everything,
feeling stays.
  As the magnolia remains,
magnificent.

✸

accordingly

  If the world ends burning,
you can all rest easy.
  All of that will end up
returning.

  Rebuild everything
per the plan of my verses.
  Wind, I said how.
Cloud, I said when.
  Sun, houses, streets,
years, ruins, kingdoms,
  I said how we were.

  Love, I said how.
And how was it, really

✸

i grabbed the five stars
from the heavens one by one
   them stars didn't come
but in my hand
   all of them
still perfume me

wings and hazards

To fly with an injured wing?
Make way when I sing.
What else have I done in life?
I did it, little one, when time
was totally on my side
and what the past they call,
nightmare, pastime,
existed for me only in books.
I did so, later on, owner of myself,
when I had to choose
between an abyss, initial glory,
and this endless story.
Wounded wing, wing
wounded,
my space, my hero.
The wing burns. To fly, pain is now zero.

raison d'être

I write. And that's it.
I write because I must,
   I must for my head spins a bit.
No one has a role in this.
   I write because there is dawn
and the stars there in the sky
   remind me of letters on paper,
when the poem has the evening drawn.
   The spider weaves its webs.
Fishes kiss and bite in season.
   And I merely write.
Does there have to be a reason?

unappearance

   Nothing resembles anything.
What would be the difference
   between the fire of my bloodline
and this red rose's inference?
   All things with their measure,
each kilometer with its kilo.
   What's the use of saying treasure,
this, yes, it's like that?
   Everything else that happens,
has never happened before.
   And even if it happened,
it soon became forgotten lore.
   Things are not the same, alike,
no possible parallel.
   We are all alone here.
You are, I am, I've been.

deadlock

It's like a lapidary thing,
some precious stones,
   glass, a darkness you bring,
haze capable of prose.
   By the skin, it is lily,
that pure delight.
   But for her, long life,
that horrible stain, slides.

suspersonas divercious

My verse, I fear, comes from the cradle.
I don't make verse because I want to,
   I verse when I converse,
and I do so for the sake of conversing.
   For what am I beyond this core,
to be twenty-four and then be seen,
   to be vice, to be versa,
to be a super-surface
   where the verb comes to be more?

I'm simply no good to observe.
I verse, persevere and preserve
   a frightful one who loses
exactly where he is.

Where could my verse be?
In some place of some place,
   where the reverse of the inverse
begins to see and to stay.
   As many proses as I pervert,
may God forbid that I should lose
   my style of verseful play.

narájow

May a fly land on the map
and land me in Narájow,
    the village whence came
the father of my father,
    the one who came to do America,
the one who will do the opposite,
    Poland as a memory,
the Atlantic up ahead,
    the Vistula in the veins.

What knows the fly of the wound
that distance cuts into raw flesh,
    when a ship leaves the port
playing the match of last resort?

Where has this map been
that only now it extends its palm
    to receive this fly
that falls into it, by mathematics?

·

ask the dust

  life grows
time grows
  everything grows
and always turns
  into this moment

  this point grows
right down the middle
  of love & its center
just the way
  what we cried
and didn't say
  grows inside

v as in voyage

  A voyage leaves me
a shallow soul,
  almost on a roll,
yet far from home.

  At home, there was life,
the journey of a marcher,
  when travelling became
a newer sleeping beauty.

  Life was on a trip
but travel wasn't my duty,
  for every voyage
is made only of departure.

To read by what's not

To read by what's not, so much better!
To sense in each absence, the strong smell
  of the body unfettered,
the thing so awaited.
  To read by what's not, beyond letters,
to see in elevated rhyme, prime stone setters,
  there, where the forms gone astray
go seek their etceteras.
  To un-read, counter-read, read-err,
to get re-entangled in these rhythms of matter,
  outside to see the inside, and inside the out,
to set sail toward the Indies
  and discover America.

Goodbye, things I've never had,
external debts, earthly vanities,
  detective loupes, goodbye.
Goodbye, unexpected plenitudes
  scares, impulses, spectacles, goodbye.
Goodbye, now off go my laments.
  One day, who knows, they will be yours,
as one day they were from my parents.
  Goodbye, mama, goodbye, papa, goodbye,
goodbye, my children, maybe someday
  all the children will be mine.
Goodbye, cruel world, paper fable,
  blowing wind, tower of babel,
goodbye, things lost out there, goodbye.

final warning

should anything happen to me,
let my family know,
    this is how it was, so it had to be

it had to be pain upon pain
this process of growing

it had to come in double
this fear of not being

it had to be a mystery
this way of mine of disappearing

a poem, for example,
should anything happen to me,
    it just might be a clue

maybe I've not yet finished writing

general aimlessness

   This strange habit,
the writing of masterpieces,
  was not a rapid process.
With rhymes the cost increases.
  For some, I paid dearly,
lyres, lives, maximum price.
  Some were clearly easy.
Others, I've no advice.
  I do still remember
one I chose to dismember.
  Two, in short.
I struck for pure sport.
  This strange abuse
I've acquired it centuries ago.
  To the others: songs to choose.
Me, sir, I'm nothing but echoes.

m as in memory

The books know by heart
thousands of poems.
What memories!
Remembrance is a valuable omen.
It's well worth the waste,
Ulysses returned from Troy,
as Dante wrote without haste,
heaven won't yield such a story.
One day the devil came through
to seduce a Doctor Faust.
As for Byron, he was true.
But Pessoa, a person, was false.
Mallarmé was so pale,
he looked more like a page.
Rimbaud to Africa went,
Hemingway mirages all spent.
Books do know about all things.
This dilemma they know to no end.
They don´t know that, down deep,
To read is no more than a legend.

*

until next time

Even you, raw material,
even you, wood, mass and muscle,
vodka, hiccups, liver,
candlelight, paper, coal and cloud,
stone, avocado flesh, rain water,
toenail, mountain, red-hot iron,
even you feel homesick and suffer,
first degree burn,
yearning to come home?

Clay, sponge, marble, rubber, cement,
steel, steam, cartilage and cloth, glass
ink, eggshell, grains of sand, ash,
first day of autumn, the word springtime,
number five, a slap in the face, perfect rhyme,
the new life, the middle ages, the old force,
even you, dear matter of mine,
remember when we were just an idea?

᭙

incense were music

this wanting
to be exactly what
we are
will still
take us beyond

✸

my gardenias and hydrangeas
do not do anything
    to remind me
I belong to this world's incidence

    please let me think
that everything is nothing
    but a terrible coincidence

What happens to water first
happens next to glory:
    no matter how much you drink,
which one quenches thirst?
    Success is different,
one verse is quite enough
    for this nasty blight
that's called to come-out-right.

poetry: 1970

    Everything I do
someone inside me whom I despise
    always thinks it's the maximum.

    My scrawl's scarcely done
and nothing can be changed.
    It's already a classic.

subject object

you will never know
homesickness' cost
the terrible burden
of carrying a city
from the very inside
how to make art of a verse
an object of a subject
how to pass from the present
to the past perfect tense
never to know hence or whence

you will never know
what comes after saturday
maybe a century
much wiser and more lovely
who knows maybe just
another sunday

you will never know
and this is wisdom
anything worthwhile
the passage to pasargada
xanadu or shangri-la
perchance the key
to a poem
and not much more

●

kawa cauim
floral disarrangements

川

KAWA

The ideogram kawa, "river" in Japanese, pictogram of a
stream of running water, always seemed to me to represent
(vertically) the scheme of the haiku, the blood of the three
lines dripping on the wall of the page...

hai

  Hark, it is born complete
and at death it dies a germ,
  this desire, illiterate,
to know my ruling concerns,
  knowing what my self does
so that I might be who I was,
  behold what's born a success
and goes on to grow even less.

ku

  Minimal temple
for a kind of smallish god,
  on guard for you here,
instead of my grieving so odd,
  my extreme vanguardian angel.

  What masks do your
boastful sorrows fancy,
  what's but vainglorious
vacancy in your story,
  whoever may know.

  It's enough, I find,
the body drawing away
  the shadow left behind.

i loved in halves full
half i have loved
half i have null

the ways i walk along
one day it will be
i can't know how long

noon   a three-colored crown
i went to say wind
all the flowers fell down

i opened an old journal
only to discover
that i once was eternal

saturdays blue the sea
i called heaven
but it was always busy

endgame,
naked,
　as i came

called me groovy,
and moved on,
　like a movie

once upon a time

the rising sun
closes my eyes
til i become japanese

a sleepless loner
dog can't stop barking
　a dream without owner

river laughs mysteriously
and where would i be
　were i taken seriously?

it rained
on the letter you sent

who sent it?

beaches   beaches   signs galore
a gaze so faraway
that look no one looks at
                                nevermore

among the boys on bikes
the very first firefly
of nineteen eighty seven

shadows
bring down
    shadows
when darkness
    then matures

shadows
the winds take
    shadows
not one
    endures

first frost of the year
i was happy
    or so it appears

        side portrait
front portrait
    make of me
someone differently

    on the church's tower
the little bird will pause
    to alight as if alighting were
the effect in the cause

    between
the water
    and the root
    b
    looms
    the
passion fruit

new year's
years in search of
new spirited ears

●

daybreak
bustle
i'll hustle my soul
for some lunch

●

rainfall

it's been a while
since i've felt
so sentimental

●

silk curtains
the wind enters
sans invitation

●

moon in sight
did you shine like this
over auschwitz?

●

tonight
as the moon beamed
  i went missing
and nobody seemed
  to feel my absence

all said,
nothing done,
  i stare and come

windy day outside
even the trees
  want to come inside

all clear and shining
it wasn´t yet day
  it was just lightning

IV. la vie en close

[1991]

l'être avant la lettre

la vie en close

c'est une autre chose

c'est lui

c'est moi

c'est ça

c'est la vie des choses

qui n'ont pas

un autre choix

[originally written in French]

being: avant la lettre
gloss + rhyme scheme

life at close	A
is another thing	A
it's him	-
it's me	B
that's it	C
it's the life of things	A
that do not have	C
another choice	B

being: avant la lettre
a version

life at close

is quite another prose

it's him

it's us

it's thus

it's the life of those

who cannot voice

another choice

●

a good poem
takes years
  five playing ball,
five more studying sanskrit,
  six carrying stone,
nine going out with a neighbor,
  seven taking a beating,
four marching alone,
  three moving from the city,
ten changing subject matter,
  an eternity, you and me,
together walk former and latter

boundaries unbound

POETRY: "words set to music" (Dante via Pound), "a voyage
to the unknown" (Mayakovsky), "gists and piths" (Ezra Pound),
"mediation of the unspeakable" (Goethe), "language focused
on its own materiality" (Jakobson), "permanent hesitation
between sound and sense" (Paul Valéry), "foundation of being
by the word" (Heidegger), "the original religion of humanity"
(Novalis), "the best words in the best order" (Coleridge),
"emotion recollected in tranquility" (Wordsworth), "science
and passion" (Alfred de Vigny), "is made with words, not with
ideas" (Mallarmé), "music made with ideas" (Ricardo Reis /
Fernando Pessoa), "a real pretense" (Fernando Pessoa),
"criticism of life" (Matthew Arnold), "word-thing" (Sartre),
"language in a state of wild purity" (Octavio Paz), "poetry is to
inspire" (Bob Dylan), "design of language" (Décio Pignatari),
"the impossible made possible" (García Lorca), "what is lost in
translation" (Robert Frost), "the freedom of my
language" (Paulo Leminski)...

●

To the one who burns me
and, burning, does reign,
   may insistence duly gain.
One day, do good turns for me.

●

ouverture la vie en close

  in Latin
for "door" one says "janua"
  and "window" is "fenestra"

  the word "fenestra"
did not come to Portuguese
  but the diminutive of "janua",
"januela", "small door", did come
  hence our word "janela"
"fenestra" came
  but not at the spot in the house
that looks out upon the world,
  from "fenestra", came "fresta",
a crevice, quite a different thing

  now in English
"janela" is the word "window"
  because through it, in comes
the cold north wind
  unless we close it
like one who opens up
  the great etymological dictionary
of interior spaces

and to view you
verdant venus
　ail aching
by skyside
　is to view us
in pure dreamland
　where to view
you, vibrant life,
　is viewing high,
via a veil

stupor

this sudden not receiving
this stupid so desiring
that leaves me inquiring
when i ought be believing

this feeling of falling
with no place existing
where you can go calling

this take it or leave it
these poems are vulgar
and none of my lies will permit

what can that be,
past far away, in the blue, quietly?

if a cloud, why does it not abate?
mountain,
how does it vacillate?

●

curitibas

I know this city well,
like the palm of my dick.
I know where the palace is,
I know where fountains click.

But I don't know of longing,
the fine flower it fabricates.
To be, I know. Who knows,
this city may mean my belonging.

●

how to shoot down a cloud

sirens, bars in flames,
cars and cars crashing,
the night calls my name,
the thing written in blood
on the walls of dance-hall sites
and of hospitals as well,
the incomplete poems
the red ever green of traffic lights

tuning in for haste and presage

I used to write in space.
Today, I graph in time,
on skin, on palms, on petals,
light of the instant.
I sound in doubts that shuffle
the ones who shout silence
apart from scandals that shuttle,
in time, distance, squares,
that pause, yes paws, take
to go from mishap to spasms.

Behold the voice, the god, the speech,
the light that was lit in the house yet
no longer fits in rooms within reach.

operation sight

From one night, I came.
For one night, we'll go pose,
   one rose of Guimaraens's
in Graciliano's boughs.

On the right Finnegans Wake,
on the left un coup de dés' quake,
   what thing can one gloss
that's not merely pure loss?

confidentiality of sources

Who is to tell of the lines
that the waves may arm and may not?
   Who is to tell of the streamers,
all the tears lit, so many candles,
   miracles, so quickly passing by?
You tell, since it is known
   that not all in the water is edge,
not everything is a cause of scandals,
   not everything tells me I love you,
not all earthly things are mirage.

Signs, shadows, images, dreamers,
no one will ever know
   how many messages they bring us.

there goes a man askew

what does he think of the night
  i don't know
i can only guess

  he thinks what anybody
thinks, no matter who

  one day
i had neighbors too

accident at km 19

  something in me fades away
something that flows

  could it be the water of life
or another good thing that grows
  so good there's no life
where this good life has no woes?

  a time when the voice of love
like voices of love echo to close?

more or less on time

Condemned to be exact,
to act vaguely I wish I could,
   will-o'-the-wisp on a lake,
deceiving all who would
   opt to fly, to swim, to fake:
mosquito, amphibian, snake.

Condemned to be exact
for scarcely a while,
   a time untracked
as if it were space,
   my exactness surprised,
rhombus, compass, tract,
   desiring what I don't desire.

                  ❧

   out there on high
the sky was making
   all the stars it could

   in the kitchen
beneath the lamp
   my mother would choose
the beans and rice
   andromeda over here
altair over there
   sirius over here
morning star over there

                  ●

seven subjects per second

Ut pictura, poesis...
          Horace

What is painting good for
save when presenting
  precisely the demand
for what it appears mostly,
  when it provides forty
enigmas times seventy?

  ●

  be still, my heart
it's still not yet again
  confusion may reign
dreaming out there

  be calm no haste
we'll enjoy it soon
  closer to the bone
better the meat may taste

(abs)

   simple
as a yes
   is simply
mind
   the most
simple thing
   that ex
ists
   so that
sim
   ply
from me
   i strip
un
   (abs)
      ent

   ˙ ⸴˙ •
   ˌ

   delays of chance
cares and concerns
   i no longer love

   what was to come
came too late
   this late date can't know
what chance is capable of

   •

surprised to be
so loose yet so captive
   about face goes the night
to pace our second plan
   all the beauty she can

⸫

mutiny inside me (1968-1988)

   xx years of x,
xx years of xerox,
   xx years of ex-chess,
i didn't seek success,
   i didn't seek failure,
my stance was seeking chance,
   this god that i undress.

seven days in the life of a light

for seven nights
a light transformed
   pain into day
a light of which I didn't know
   whether it came along with me
or had been born all by itself

for seven days
a light shone
   in the burn unit
burned the pain
   burned the lack
burned all that comprised
   what had to be cauterized

miracle beyond sin
what sense can be devised
   to have more meaning?

Hospital S. Vicente
Burn Unit
Curitiba, October 1987

with how many paulos

paulos paulos paulos
how many paulos do you need
to make a são paulo

ditties ages ditties
how much gives a soul
divided by two cities?
; ⋯ •
, •

a time like that
only the very first year
i barely could cry
one entire tear

let go tearful thirst
the first one to see
that january's moon
is the day april first

; ⋯ •
•

in honore ordinis sancti benedicti

to the order of St. Benedict
the order that knows
that fire is slow
and out here does go
the order that goes inside

the order knows
that everything is holy
the hour the color the water
the chant the incense the silence
and inside the smallest trace
there opens up profoundly
the immense flower of space

uneven or odd

I rarely rhyme so much with before.
I'd sooner rhyme men with when,
   seeking less with more.
I rhyme, you rhyme, you look, we roar,
   as if we all rhymed,
as if we all laughed,
   as if loving (rhyming) were easy.

Life, a thing to be depicted,
as is this fate that violates me.
   Once I say it, my wisdom is conflicted
with the infinite schism that dilates me.

someone standing erect
others will always suspect
   of nesting as I nest
a fright stuck in the chest,
   a deadline, a pleasure, to sever,
a deed done however,
   subject to being ingested
by the first one invested

   standing up brings bad luck

one who comes out like his own

  more voices
fewer voices
  the machine in us
that generates proverbs
  is the same that makes poems,
sums with their very own lives
  that can do more than we can

paramounts of quintessence

  The role is short.
Living is long.
  Occult or odd-leaning,
all that I say
  has ultra-meaning.

  If I laugh at me,
take me seriously.
  Sterile irony?
In the interim goes
  my infra-mystery.

Walking and thinking a bit,
I can only think when walking.
   Three steps taken, my legs are
already thinking wit.

   Where will all these steps lead?
Upstairs or down?
   Beyond? Or perchance on pace
to fall apart in minimal wind
   leaving nary a trace?

                    ⁖

   you're so far away
that sometimes i think
   that i just don't exist

   don't even talk of love
for love, it is this

             ●

cinema lights

the cinema your destiny
the film FEEL ME
  signeme
        hold me firmly

  cinema show me
to be yes
      and to be a stream

  countless times i have the will
that changing things never should
  turnaroundturnback
to change is all i could

  this world has been lost
dispersed 'tween what's written
  and the spirit noise crossed
'tween physical and the chemical
  flows all sense, liquid cost

  life's quite a showing
because i do miss you
  since i'm dragging around
still this false issue
  my crooked soul
and the longing fakes out
  but comes back
amidst comings and goings

fixed stars

Here hundreds sensing
the sanctions that suit them.
   Scene by scene feeling
and someone remembered a poem
   that reminded him of someone.

Thousands of rhymes, vertigos twisting,
thus do I feel the fears of existing.
   If this verse exists for real,
I no longer need to feel.

●

round about midnight

a suspicious shadow guest
and the jumping of a scare
   let loose within the chest

in the dead-end alley
pathways at random
   the range of chasms
between an echo
   and its allies

[original title in
English]

dunce upon a time

i never make the same mistake
twice
  i go ahead and make it three
four five six times
  until this error learns
that only errors have their turns

How I wish I were a musician
who played only the classics,
  audience in tearful rendition
and me counting measures.
  If I had known now,
as I found out in advance,
  the allegorical dance
between all vowels and consonants!

Dear Lord who promised
eternal life to St. Benedict's children
  thank you for the winters in the wind
and for the invention of hell
  still here on this earth

on route to the root

Fake it, people are looking.
Some look up to the sky,
   galaxies, comets, moons.
Others look sideways,
   lunettes, syntax, moonlight.
Aside, head on, hooking,
   there's always people looking,
looked at or looking.

Others, yes, they look down,
searching for some trace
   of the time that we find,
looking for lost space.
   Rare the folks who look inside,
since nothing there resides.
   Only an immense burden,
the soul, this fairy tale.

●

transtwilight

      tempest
that might pass
   leaving the petals intact
you passed through me
   your wings spread open
      you passed
   but i still feel a pain
at the exact point of the body
where your shadow touched
what flash of hurt is this
   the greater the pain
   brighter shines the sun?

●

page oh page maternal home
where i always stay amazed
always meek in whiteness glazed
when entering a cave or dome

texts texts texts

damn phoenician plates
covered with scratched scratches
how you kept my eyes as matches
mind malicious twisted fate
patches

●

piece of pleasure
perdition in an obscure
  corner of the dark room
paradiso inferno
  dead or alive
i procure you

with velocity
as the voice itself
  link and duel
  between her and me
turning us and turning we

the splendid steed
sees the shadow of the whip
and runs, splendors of the horse
in mazes of mane
encouraged by the wind
cancels spaces of chimera
consuming time
pyre that heroes incinerate
it had heavenly impetus
and eagerness on the sea
the cerulean fields of the poles
the sky pelt of a jaguar
and zodiac slides
painful fields of the open ocean
where fishes graze
and octopus knots slaughter the sun
Here the fable fails
in the seasickness of waveplay
wounds the hooves in the stars
and stung by the edges
of the beasts of the horoscope
it becomes a bit blurry
the waking falls in the dream
lucid and sudden since a martyr
It stays on the ground, stallion
the eyes full of stars
the body clown of the waves
and the heart in the chest
like a whipping-top asleep!

the late arrivals
slowly must pace
  pace like rivals
who depart for no place

  life that vents me
fate that breezes me
  only he who needs you
invents you too

      ⋯ •
       •

om/ zaúm for roman ossipovitch jakobson

EU

The world was collapsing around you,
as you sought out the soul hidden
  in the heart of the syllable YES.
  Consonant? Vowel? A train to Oslo.
Pairs, contrasts, Moscows, transmental tongues.
  In the Nordic night, a rabbi, Viking,
dreams of skies with occlusives and bilabials ridden.

RO

A world, the old world, fall tree forbidden,
Hitler enters Prague, Russia, revolutzia,
  until never more!
  The Czech labiovelar
to the Urals goes unbidden.

PE

Rome, Roman, romantic pomegranate,
Jak, Jakob, Jakobson, Jacob's son grown,
  to preserve the words of men.
  As long as there is a phoneme,
I'll never be alone.

things
do not
begin with a hop
nor do they end with a .

●

donna mi priega 1988

wisemen discuss
if love is an exchange
  or deliverance to arrange
between smaller strips
  and all the thicker lips

  in the first case
where does chance have its base
  and purpose its end
if everything we do
  is less than love
but hate can't yet contend?

  the thesis that follows
as a question gets hollow
  and deliverance is so crazy
that all waiting is lazy?
  which of the five thousand senses
is free of misunderstood offenses?

don't forget to look like me

   this wasn't here yesterday
a poor day was yesterday, half,
   begging for gold
from the misery, eternally old

   today is a day of riches
a world full of light and tears
   force flower miraculous risks

   today looks at itself in the mirror
and it only seems like yesterday
   the same breeze the identical mist
and this intense fog
   that forces us to close our eyes
and read under between the lines
   these abysses of mine and of ours
   today, indeed, it's a wonder,
finally, today, i do not know

mother's day / 1988

R
(light years, darkness-years) *

To read, review all,
and between the V and the L
to view that last
ar-may-R
err
to reve(reverie)al me

* Read darkness. In letters, read everything you do not dare to read. Read more. Read beyond. Beyond good. Beyond evil. Beyond the beyond. Overtime or etcetera, goodbye, amen. Let others seek the speed of light. I seek the speed of darkness.

tout est déjà dit
dans un jardin
        jadis

fernando uma pessoa
j'ai perdu ma vie

par deicatesse?
oui
    rimbaud
moi
  aussi

            ⁖   [originally written in French]

all is already said
in a garden
       long ago

fernando one pessoa
i've lost my life

for delicacy?
yes
    rimbaud
me
    too

            ⁖

blade runner waltz

In nineteen eighty and forever,
ah, those were the days,
  we danced by moonlight, to the sound of the waltz
The Perfection of Love through Pain and Renunciation,
  a name, I confess, a little too long,
but the times, those times,
  ah they no longer make times
like they used to.
  Those really were hours,
enormous days, year-long weeks, minutes millennia,
  and all that fortune by the way
we spent doing silly things,
  loving, dreaming, dancing to the sound of waltzes,
those false waltzes with such long slow names
  that we danced on some september
in those nineteen eighties and forever.

●

All is vague and very varied,
my destiny has no wisdom,
  what I want has no price,
a price possessed cannot be buried,
  nothing needed nor precise.

voyage au bout de la nuit

the breast bruised with veracity
i roll on the street this bald and blinded head
no longer good for the devil who carries it ahead

phantom opera

I have nothing.
Nothing from me can be taken.
I'm the ex-stranger, the one
who came though no one called
and, feline, got around
making nary a sound.

profession of fever

when it rains,
i rain,
if there's sunshine
i shine,
at night,
i fall,
if there's a god
i pray,
if there's not,
i forget,
it rains again
again, i rain,
whistle in a groove,
i see myself from here,
there i go,
gesture on the move

Seven twenty-one.
Here lies the sun,
  shade at my feet.

Darkness is nigh.
What else to be read
  by a poet with pride?

water into water

  their asking for a miracle
not even a brisk blink
  i'll turn water into water
and risk into risk

  This life of a hermit,
sometimes rife with empty.
  At times a visit on hold.
At times it just gets cold.

at the feet of a painful pen

all dirty with ink
the scribe returns home
headful of lines ill-gotten
pat phrases
letters of ire
lovely verses
the skin on fire
the words forgotten
apes shapes
all the words of the tribe

for them
he traded his life
days lights dawns
today
when home he remembers
blank page and in embers
wing there he goes
face to face without strife
with everything inside
he departs

aurora on alpha

   all the weight
to measure myself
   i view and envy
and in this vast vista
   i let myself go fending
'til i can't see anything else
   dis-comprehending

   what i saw
was long-viewing and pure

   whom i viewed
will view

   only what's becoming will
             come
and in what's viewing will be
             come

the alphabet animal
has twenty-three paws
   or nearly

   wherever it goes
words and phrases
   clearly are born

   with phrases
wings are made
   and words
wind will unwind

   the alphabet animal
goes on its way
   the unwritten stays behind

   a man with something wrong
is much more courtly
   sideways he walks
as if by arriving shortly
   he'll make it farther along

   he carries the weight of the pain
as if displaying medals
   a crown one-million dollars
or something in that vein

   opioids edens analgesics
don't you touch this pain of mine
   it's all that i have left
suffering to be my ultimate sign

tibagi

stuck in time
the moon
    over there
as if forever

the green
    right there
fulfilling its duty

just to be green
until it can't be seen

down with beyond

during the day
cloudy skies
    or heaven astray

at night
not having clouds
    stars
always have their way

oh what a treat
an empty sky
    blue exempt
of sentiment
    and animal heat

this really does haunt and delight me:
how does a hark! penetrate the darkness
and an owl escape from the owl-light?

Death, we celebrate.
In my breast, a Rome falls,
   that, fallen away,
no barbarian stalls.

The pomegranates that we may eat
and the splendors of the person,
   improper terms upon the sheet,
whomever it hurts, pain may worsen.

the ex-stranger

   a passenger alone
the heart as a target,
   always the same, now overblown,
saggitarius sign, the arrow is thrown,
   at the galaxy's one central zone

tombstone 1
epitaph for the body

A great poet here lies.
Nothing written could he leave.
    This calm silence, I believe,
his complete works shall comprise.

                ⠂⠂•
                •

tombstone 2
epitaph for the soul

here lies an artist
master of disasters

living
with the intensity of art
    led him to a heart attack

    may god have pity
on all his disguises

                ●

    may my memory evaporate
like some water
    so tearfully

    may my remembrance be gone
without leaving any other
    in its proper place

    if i one day should forget
that you will never forget me

dismantling
the love machine
 piece by piece
where flowery flowers have sheen
 leaving nothing nor promise
yes this i would not cease
 to do if i could
make my prayer
 a cold stone affair

 ⋰•
 •

 such bitter pain
the poor weeping sustains

 why the hell then
don't you come here

 if there's so much rain?

 ●

mini-funeral-prayer for rené descartes

 Bene vixit qui bene latuit*

 Here under the slab does rest
the one who lived occult.
 Spare him the outrageous test
of all tumult.

* "He who lived out of sight, lived well", Descartes' motto.
(Author's Note)

 ●

what's gone down, is gone down?

Formerly, people would die.
1907, let's say, yes sir,
that really was dying.
Every day people would die,
and they did so with pleasure,
since everyone knew why
the Judgment Day, at last, would come,
and every soul would be reborn.
People died per every rule and measure.
Of illness, of childbirth, of cough.
And they even died of love,
as if loving were a death.
In order to die, a fright was enough,
a hanky in the wind, a sigh and done,
our dearly departed was gone
buried underground with his boots on.
Day of years, marriage, baptism,
dying was a party, excitement,
one of the things in life,
like not to be or to be invited.
Scandal was standard fare.
The damage, a minimal mess.
He's gone, at rest. May he be with God.
Someone always had a phrase
that left it more or less.
There were things that fatally sealed.
Cucumber with milk, channeled wind,
curse of old women and love badly healed.

There were things that just had to die,
there were things that had to be killed.
    One's honor, the land and our blood
sent many to their final resting place.
    What more could an old man do,
in the year of 1916,
    other than catch pneumonia,
leave everything on his sons' behalf
    and turn into a photograph?
No one held a life-long bond.
    After all, life is so short.
He just couldn't go beyond.
    But no one is to blame.
Who told him better not be a devotee
    of St. Ignatius of Acapulco,
The Infant Jesus, scourge of Prague?
    The devil, folks, is running free.
Here you do it, here you pay for it.
    He had lunch and shaved,
took a shower and off to the windy chill.
    There's nothing to complain about.
Now, to commence reading the will.
    Today, death is difficult.
There are resources, asylums, remedies.
    Now death has limits.
And, in case of necessity,
    the science of eternity
invented cryonics.
    Today, indeed my friends, life is chronic.

who is
worried
about this
beyond
in no hurry
?

to me
the bond of
a turn

the
beyond
to
whom
it may
concern

one could spend
one's entire life like this
gazing at the moon
a mouthful of light
and on one's head no trace
of the word glory

extra

   precise surprise
passing breeze leaves me bright eyes
   wing that couldn't be a star
second screen foiled
   speech dissolved in prayer
rose in honey boiled

   overnight beyondforest
that star is a thorn
   through which i see a new sky
       set to be born

       ●

     forgetfulness will one day fall
all over us as well
   like the rain on the roof
and us being forgotten
   will almost be happiness

       ●

mourning for my own self

the light sets down
in every atom of the universe
   nighttime absolute
this evil our illness acute
   as if every atom's plight
as if this were the ultimate fight

   the style of this pain
it's a classic
   it hurts in all the right places
without leaving traces
   it hurts nearby it hurts faraway
with nothing left behind
   it hurts in himalayas, in interstices
as well as in the low lands

   a pain that in joyfulness rose
as if hurting were poetic
   since everything else is prose

Make the right gestures,
destiny will ally with you,
   I hear a voice saying on cue
from the deepest depths of the past.
   Today, I don't do anything right,
for it takes much more pride
   to do nothing at all per the guide.

   Woe to chance, too,
should it not stay on my side.

travelling life

(for Bere)

   it's as if it were a warring scheme
where a bad goat battles
  and a good goat doesn't scream

   it's as if it were a land
foreign even to its own band
  as if it were a screen
where every film being seen
  would freeze the image at hand

   it's as if it were the beast
that every day does spin and roll
  to more and more reveal its role

[original title in English]

plenty of love

when i saw you
i had an idea so fecund
it was as if i were looking
from well within a diamond
and my eyes reckoned
with a thousand faces in a second

it takes just a second
voilá you have plenty of love

light vs. light

from illusion to illusion
until the disillusion
it's a step sans solution
an embrace

an abyss
several
sighs
farewell to all that is good

he who seems to be sane is not
and those who don't seem so, gain

killing, the highest form of loving,
killing in us the will to kill,
return to killing the will,
killing, always, killing,
even if, for this,
one may need all our loving

turns vs. downturns

a flash back
a flash back inside a flash back
a flash back inside a flash back of
a flash back
a flash back inside the third flash back
the memory falls into the memory
stoneflower on smooth water
everything tires (flash back)
except the memory of the memory of the memory
of the memory

haja
hoje
p/
tanto
houtem

p.l

to - do
to - day
for
so much
yisterday

só
o
e
isto
ex
ist

pleminski
88

only
the
ex
it
ex
ists
p leminski
88

only
the (I)
ex
this (ist)
ex
ist(s)]

obra

cobra
dobra
manobra
obra
sobra
V. a f. dos v. em
    obrar : desdobra.

From an antique rhyming dictionary, a ready-made
concrete poem: work (œuvre)- snake / fold / maneuver
/ work / leftover / Cf. singular conjugations of like
verbs.

Leminski might conceive something like:

work
berk
clerk
irk
jerk
lurk
murk
perk
quirk
shirk
smirk
twerk

downpour

try to look down pour out your thunder til nothing remains but wonder

expect	no	amaze	ment
from	my	insis	tence
spoken	at	dis	tance
a maze	of	tongues	hence

●

anfíbios

a pena chama	a chama vela a pena chama a vela pena	a chama traça a vela a traça vela a pena	a traça vara a parte lança a chama parte	a lança vara a chama traça a vara vela
a dura dita chama a pena dura	a vela sua a chama vela a sua chama	a dita dura vela a dura vara	a pena pára para para para	a chama pena

a pena = the plume (n.) | pena = grieves (v.)

chama = calls (v.) | a chama = the flame

a dura = the hard one | dura = endures (v.)

dita = good fortune | dita = dictates (v.)

(ditadura = dictatorship)

pára = stops (v.); para = (in order) to

a vela = the candle | vela = veils (v.)

sua = sweats (v.); a sua = its (poss.)

a traça = the moth; traça = traces (v.)

vara = shafts (v.) | a vara = the shaft

a parte = the part; parte = departs (v.)

a lança = the lance; lança = lances (v.)

amphibians

(homographic homonyms)

the plume calls	the flame veils the plume calls the candle grieves	the flame traces the candle the moth veils the plume	the moth shafts the part lances the flame departs	the lance shafts the flame traces the shaft veils
the hard fortune calls the plume hard	the candle sweats the flame veils its flame	fortune hard veils the hard shaft	the plume stops to to to	the flame grieves

from haicai [haiku], cai = falls

kawázu

"Kawázu" is "frog" in Japanese. I imagine it was originally related to "kawa", "river". The batrachian is the totemic animal of haiku, ever since that memorable moment when Master Basho witnessed how a frog "tobikomu" ("jump-enters") into the old pond, the sound of water.

mallarmé basho

a leap of a frog
will never abolish
 the ancient pond

five bars, ten cognacs
i traverse são paulo
 asleep inside a taxi

this flight straight
to the most painful wind
 i donate

a kiss pleasing taste
             of swordfish
way out there
       the water must be freezing

when it gets dark
all that is lacking
 may embark

the castle
that the general could not conquer
   the shadow of the afternoon woods
                              could

seeing is violent

what stroke
to make the wind silent?

   take knowledge in stride

how does sea water
   get inside the coconuts?

   municipal cemetery
peace and calm reign
   throughout the national territory

   heat and hot breeze
he who needs you
   foresees

this highway can go far
but if it really goes
it will be greatly missed

what could there be
down under there
that the stone falls
so easily?

things of the wind
the hammock swings
with no one in it

i leer at shooting stars
the sky has departed
for a solo career

what i'd most like to hear
even for flowers in the vase
one day spring will be here

vacuum acute

i live like i won't

i don't give a hoot

long-hanging fruit
to what kind of fright
might i belong?

everything grooving
hosted at houses
that also are moving

greyness at dawn
the way i get up
   this way i'll get down

startling
draws abstract assault
   my shadow on asphalt

new tiles
upon first rain
   new leaks and drips

love is a link
between the blue
   and the pink

old photos
old and retold
   a lotus flower

long the path to heaven
my errant soul wasting
   tasting like a hotel room

insular

a thousand miles of darkness
surrounded by wailing
from all tides

the parakeet has died
the empty cage
hides cries of rage

this life is trippy too
such a pity i'm just
passing through

the long path warns
of leading to a flower
all made of thorns

so disgusting take
from you i remake
a soul still in pieces

day without sense
i light cigarettes
in the incense

what makes

the southern cross

so low?

the lights of my street

i suppose

vertigo
with   me
seeing you go

in a sea of people
i left untread
my steps ahead

the day is in shambles
the flight of the doves
over their own shadows

                            winter
                    all i feel is distinct
                        and to live
                        is succint

                    what day is today?
                    one day i could say
                    today it escapes me

from esperanto to wonder
through ex-weeping and thunder
for the time being under

high night   low moon
soon ask the frog
what's croaking's tune

springtime of problems
the light of grand flowers
bemuses mere blossoms

●

crescent moon
the darkness grows
the stars swoon

●

the work is done
the wind is blowing
there's time for fun

●

sunset   drop of blood
honey-fragranced flower in milk-colored water
awakens the fish
dreams of phosphorous

●

to spin a web in one minute
the spider charges so little
just one mosquito

●

naked as a greek
i hear a black musician speak
and to disaggregate i seek

●

very romantic
my pacific point
   is in the atlantic

believe it or not
this very if
  is everything you got

                    [originally written in English]

night – large and deep
everything asleep
  save the name you keep

the crow swims in gold
the sky spoils not the flight
  the flight damns not the sky

        ,

it rains on dew now
the key of the door
  like a flower on a bough

happy the slug in may
a rainy day lift
  as a birthday gift

don't try to array my mess
no ship much less a train
  will lead me to a new address

i understand
but i don't understand
  what i'm understanding

"fuck it all",
she said like a pup,
  and got all fucked up

tatami it or leave it

from mattress to mattress
i found as i roam
  the floor is my home

wee morning hours   open bar
there must be some mistake
              not too far

formerly is ancient
wine rains as sleet
              over fields of wheat

midnight
silence clinks
  shadows become scenes
and dreams cinematic links

moons too much ado
errata: for one
  please read two

this is the life i want,
oh so fine

to lean your wound
all against mine

star   lone sign
suddenly   a voice
   speaking within mine

●

   so early, and grinning
so now
   all anew is beginning

●

   i saw lives, i saw deaths,
nothing i saw could measure
   up to the bad luck i had
by having you, my treasure

         ●

   i do now and then
go walk walk walking
   my voice echoing talk
of when when when

●

   clean moon
at the edge of the abyss
   all things are so simple

●

I've made a deal with my body.
Never get sick.
　When you do want to die,
I'll let you go.

♠

　　　life and death
love and doubt
　　　　pain and knack

　　　those mad enough
let them come back

♠

the party is over
the ants use their choppers
　on remains of grasshoppers

♠

　i end up as i began
songs without wits
　are no longer hits

♠

ain't no saint

no saint
saint no
   pray for us
not to be
   but so

my soul oh so brief
the lightest element in
   the table of mendeleev

this here idea
no one can deny
matter is a lie

V. the ex-stranger

[1996]

This book of poems, which was going to be called *The ex-stranger*, expresses, in most of the poems, a life experience of dépaysement, the discomfort of not-belonging, the discontent of the out-of-focus, the most modern of feelings. In this, perhaps, its sole modernity is enciphered.

p. leminski

the ex-stranger

invernacular
(3)

Anyone can see that
this language isn't mine.
When meaning walks free,
the word must stay behind.
Maybe I barely swear lies,
perhaps I just lie truth.
So I say to myself, minimally,
who knows, I feel, maybe a sleuth.
This language is not mine.
The language I speak blurred
distant song and wine,
the voice, beyond, not even a word.
The dialect one utilizes
on the left bank of the phrase,
that's my speech of luso-sizes,
me, in half, me, inside, me, agaze.

●

I've said it of us.
I've said it 'bout me.
I've said it of the world.
I've said it now,
who have also said never.
Everyone knows,
I've said quite a lot.

I have the impression
that I've said it all.
And it was all so sudden.

●

disaster of an idea
only the during endures
    what the days ahead delay

    strange forms life has proffered
when i eat everything i am offered
    with naught my satisfaction ever stays

    strange shapes hunger may assume
when the day is disorder
    and my sleepy dreams plume

    hunger from china hunger from india
hunger that has yet to take color
    his rage that desires
        whatever it may bloom

i am rime-able and we are risible

Parnassian avian,
I never rhyme so much is in store.
 I quickly rhyme then with when,
thus seeking less with more.
 I rhyme, you rhyme, you look, we laugh,
as if we all indeed were rhyming,
 as if we all indeed were laughing,
if loving were so easy.

 Asked why I rhyme in so many pieces
reply that a rhyme is such a rare thing.
 The rare, in a rarefied way, ceases,
as it halts, without anger, any singing.
 To rhyme is to stop, to stop look and listen
to the rummage in the bottom of the conch
 with that still unfinished honk,
Pompeii, idea, Vesuvius,
 seas speaking only of seas that glisten.

 Life, a thing to be narrated,
as to death I am with fortune fated.
 Barely do I say it and my saying so conflicts
with all the schism, malediction, to kick my fix.

how should i know?

the desire despair to come back
goes through the shadows, so steady,
  before i'm even ready
to commit the crime on track,
  to turn myself into another
or as another my self disarm
  perhaps an artwork, a brother
how should i know, perhaps a false alarm,
  to fall down the well, screaming yes
in this wee well i see and hear nothing,
  more more and more
each time less and more brittle

  being able, i feel, is all i can,
all that we can do is so little

lactose, lectures,
literature, letters,
  everything that passes,
everything that lasts
  everything that hardly passes
everything that lastly endured
  everything, everything, everything,
is nothing but a caricature
  of you, my bitterness inured
to seeing that living has no cure

the noise of them sawing
the noise of someone washing clothes
  sound like the weeping of those who weep
for a life that can't suffice
  it even seems that now's the time
to stand up high
  and see that life
will never be another

Round. No, it will never be round
this crazy life of mine
  my four-sided life,
square and quatrain,
  no, all is in vain,
this life will not be mine.

  Life broken in half or more,
you never said what you came for.

at the moment of meanwhile

  say my poetry
and forget me should you endeavor
  move on and then tell me
who won that quarrel
  between how much and whatever

olinda wischral

people should be able to evaporate
whenever they want
and not leave around
memories pieces carcasses
drops of blood skulls skeletons
and that tightness in the chest
that will not let me sleep

take for bere

it was all very sudden
all very frightening
all like the replies
when the question arrives

this half issue of whether
when we are far faraway
yet continue together

happy coincidence

any coincidence
is mere resemblance
  while the quixote hatches ideas
sancho scratches his paunches

  may all things be equal
may the red be green
  and blue as yellow be seen
and always be nevermore

●

  this planet is sometimes tiring,
black souls, faces white with ire
  nights of battle inspiring,
soiled watery eves can't aspire,
  minutes of dread and power

  house full of sweets,
waves clinking with pain,
  former bitterness now to cower,
set foot on this planet
  as one who crushes a flower

●

mixture of boredom and mystery
half day / half way
  splinter of doubt seen in winter
fear possessed by the night
  may the day earlier awake
and dawn an eternity take

azure like the smiles of children
and heavy like the proverbs of old ladies
  for years i cultivated the idea of the poem,
whole thing, many eggs, eagerness, antennae,
  my poems are ideas
yesterday, something whole, today, only stains

my brazilian self

  i wish i could think
as is done in the old world
  they want me to be a mirror
as if there were no mystery
  in my lack of subject matter

for some of the nights that we've been having

let me open the door
i wanna see if night's going well

maybe the moon is mooning
or in dreams children
shadows amen quietly yell

let's see who fades away first
the cloud the star or no one can tell

●

i never know for certain
if i'm a doubting boy
or a man of true faith

certainties with wind fleet
only doubts can stand on their feet

●

how momentous

our lady of light
gold from our bethlehem river
may this day be eternal
as long as shadows don't quiver

●

to all those who love me
or have loved me one day
    i leave just a lord's prayer
half medium rare
    and this sort of hailstorm mary

●

hieroglyph

All things are there
to enlighten us.
    When the disciple is ready,
the master appears,
    immediately,
in the form of a critter,
    in the shadow of hymns,
under a common appeal
    as in a book, slowly.

The master at the wheel,
we customarily waver,
    ignoring if critters can feel
what we people savor
    when ending thought's ordeal.

●

hexagram 65

For the damage, not a tear.
All damage is blessed.
  From the most malignant year,
is born the best beautiful day.

1 day,
  1 month, 1
    year.
/

dionysus ares aphrodite

to the gods of cruelest term

  eternal youth

they give us to drink

  in the same goblet

wine, blood and sperm

de tertulia poetarum

de tortura militum
libera nos domine
de nocte infinita
libera nos domine
de morte nocturna
libera nos domine

amorous: arms under the altar

for brother betto and brother leonardo boff

holy are the people
when it's cold outside
  and warm inside, peaceful
– come in! I say,
  time to be equals,
time to be different,
  between you and enter

sacro lavoro

the hands that write this line
were one day set to be a priest's
transforming bread and wine of feast
into flesh and blood of christ the lord

today they transform words to strike
accords between the obvious and the unexplored

What tomorrow doesn't know,
yesterday never knew.
Nothing other than today
ever came through.

typing this text

reading can be read in fingers
not in one's eyes
for eyes are more given
to secretive things

a thousand and one nights until babel

Tower
whose fall
  became legend,
to this day,
  the shadow,
as a member,
  remembers.

johnny b. good

  there are times when i desire
that nothing should change
  i go check
and change is all i could arrange

dwelling well
dwelling faraway
  dwelling there where
my farthest when
  does dwell

twisted tongue (2)

my ears
can't believe my eyes

  the water falls
bet the fire
        flies

[originally written in English]

as much as i twirl
nothing in me can imagine
  what such a little girl
can possibly be doing
  in this big city swirl

i woke up to look at myself in the mirror
still in time to glare
  at my dreams becoming nightmares

art that shelters you your art habitation
art that you lack art your imitation
art that models you art your meditation
art that dwells in you art your contexture
art that is all of you art your pretexture
art that walls you in your ART KEY TEXTURE

  flesh   soul
form   content
  all over us
the shadowy whole

S.O.S.

  i couldn't say a single yes
that wasn't the start
  of an s. o. s.

                    re
            smote
remote   eras
        a thousand
            &
            one
            moats

regret
only
one
 time

october
on the roof avian vias
 raindrops

living is surfeit hard
the deepest
 is always on the surface

Darkness is nigh.
What else to be read
  by a poet with pride?

  off they go so far
one fine day, the pyramids of egypt
  are going to reach the stars

  in the center
the encounter
  between my silence
and the thunder

  after much thought
i've decided to publish
everything the heart
says that i ought

de-part from LO/VE

unvestige

olfactory or factual
the breeze brings
a falsified smell

an old brilliancy
here to play with me
that years ago fell

1988
(upon the passage of the constellation alice)

●

to a plumed letter
one shall not respond
in truth no answer is better
something like as if the wave
did not end up as foam
such something like loving
were more than fog's rave

a something so complex
as if a rainy day
were an open parasol
as if, ah, as if,
of how many as ifs
is this story called
you and me made

1988

●

scrap yard

nostalgia for a future that never was
the one that would be noble and yet poor
how could all that have
become this present power
and this canned despair?

yes, it could, as it still can
all we've always allowed to be able
so much surprise foreseen
to die caught in the wounded throat
reasoning that ended up in prayer
feast day that today we inter

yes it can, it always can, like everything ours
that we allow to be able and no power mars

1987

1987, have mercy on us

  odd years
are victim years
  years thirsty
for blood and revenge
  punishment for every pleasure
and the desert as inherited measure

  odd years
are measles reflex pains chicken pox
  mouths that practice
cue sticks and shards of tongues
  trash where memory dwells

  the rules change, the map changes,
change in the entire trajectory
  in an odd year,
what doesn't change is our history

1987

  my friend's garden plants
everybody's happy
  even all the ants

1978

ah if at the very least
i could love you less
everything would be much easier
the days more amenable
leaves from inside the lettuce

but no
there had to be between us
this fire
this iron
this quarry
extremes
calling extremes in the distance

1976

Loving you is a matter of minutes
Death is less than your kiss
It's so good being yours as I am
Me spilled at your feet I lay down
There's little left of what I was
On you depends being good or bad
I'll be as you find convenient
I'll be for you more than a canine
A shadow to leave you in sweats
A god who does not forget
A servant who says no other
Your father dead, I'll be your brother
I'll say verses you want and prefer
I'll forget other women and her
I'll be everything and everyone
You'll feel sick when I'm this nervous
And there I'll be at your service
As long as my body lasts
While something flows in my veins
The red river that's igniting
When I see your face as a torch
I'll be your king bread thing and porch
Yes, I will be here

1968

●

1.

Animals oversee the vault,
constellations are signs.
There is no hint of stars,
the comets - so solemn,
the moon - an enigma.
Celestial bodies - in contact,
hard light of their high hierarchy.

2.

- The stars are indocile,
today, Lord,
the sky is closed. Voices of patrons
speak low.
Nobody will force the Zodiac.
Mars is covered with shields.
The moon is very dirty,
you should believe in everything,
stars murmur.
Rebellious is Mercury,
I know nothing of Saturn.

My art, for today, shall be quiet
You be quiet, Lord, as life rolls
around your fist.
Witness am I.

1974

VI. winterverno

[2001]

W   (WIND)   (WE)
        INTER   (I INVENT)
                              (INTERVIEW)
MOVE TO VISIT YOU
                              (INTERN)
        (HOVER)   IN THE   (NIGHT)
        (TENDER)   **WINTERTIME**   (NERVE)
        (NEVER)   (INVERT)   (NEVER MORE)

liberty
a wind
  where everything
        fits

miracle
the teardrop
    stops

that's it
it's all done
  my point won

between stone and stone
leave no stone
  unturned

there behind
there will be
  what i find

there we go again
reading without choice
  the one same voice

the hour of the tiger

a tiger
  when it entigers
is no flower
  to be smelt
is no tiger
  to be felt

  being a tiger
an entire life
  to be dealt

  month without end
does it come from outside
  or from within
this fragrance
  of jasmine?

I've kept all that I amassed.
Everything for which I asked.
  What once was mine
will never be past.

steps on the moist sand
from the villages - the last one by
  even whores seem strangely shy

IT IS AND IT IS

  Diamonds endure
inside the pure stone.
  Now from now on
enduring is on its own.

hail oh wind
full of grace
hail
to all that's apace

bitches' bar
the days are not many
 the nights are aplenty

　　　●

 will i go far?
and where?
 just ask
the cable car

 here
i do
 what everyone
does
 whatever i do
anything goes

　　●

 light at night
darkness
took off

time's getting tight
everything terse
getting
                    worse

                    ●

All is cut short
except what is lovely
    Idée fixe
is my favorite sport

                    ●

my wish to be
the more i look
    the less i see

on the sudden table, plain,
the bunch of grapes
    hears the steps of the rain

                    ●

heard the latest?
rain washed away
    my guilty basis

whatever smoke
matter does
what matter
may stoke

the corn is right
next time
the rain
    might fall
      near this site

i awaken
from here to there
easy to take in

my problem

only hurts

when it burns

wind we resent too
don't you exist
  we'll invent you

    there inside
what is it there
  that here outside
there's nobody left?

    such pure delight
the wave breaking
  like fruit all ripe

    Before evening dawns
and night turns into day
    put poetry in the coffee
and coffee in the poetry

    carnival passes
kept in a cask
  your half mask

.

VII. scattered poems

[1983-89]

vain is everything
that's not pleasure
pleasure shared
between partners

vain
all things gone fain

so
high
the
tower

even
its
fall
became
legend

henchantment

with so much doing nothing
i've just been blamed for everything

expectations, i arrived
too late like a teardrop

from so much making everything
                    look perfect
you can go crazy
or for all effects
suspect
of being a verb with defective subject

think a little
drink a lot
then tell me all you detected

whoever it may be
is wishing
that it may happen otherwise
at whatever cost tomorrow
to have a calendar of sorrows
to celebrate
so much avoiding the inevitable
in vino veritas
seems to me
to be the truth

the wood in life
the vinegar
smooth wine
think and may you find it apt
if not i'll invent you for all eternity

no
  god
    hindu
      ogum
        vishnu
needs
  your prayer

your haste
      person
only your pulse
        accelerates

you suffer
what's left for you
        is suffering

everything
    one fine day
        fades away

langu
age Qua
si Chi
ne
  se

this langu (age) Ming
          les
            Jin
              gles

damned be
he who doesn't let one sing
the singing is weak

damned be
he who doesn't let one sing
the singing is strong

damned be
he who doesn't let one sing
the singing begets more singing

damned be
he who doesn't let one sing
the singing never lets singing down

i saw the sun squared
sun with eyes flared
multiplied by the sun

turn on the lamp at six in the evening
turn on the lamp light
ignite
    the flame of the halls
    dragon tongue fires
    fireflies

in a cloud of neon dust
all is clear
      all is clear
      the night like this is dear

the light shining on the window at home
the fire
    the focus there in the alley
                    and the
traffic light

tonight the sun will shine

s

oun

d

ors

o

nic

o

rso

s

i(y)g

n

ony

m

undergroundblitzkrieg

the close-up of the souvenir
the ersatz of the harakiri
the marketing of pindorama

à la mao

the pine tree
has grown
    beside the tree
    with yellow flowers
it
me
    you
    she

those who pass by
    feel

      flowers are
      from one

        not the
        other

●

clean aquarium water
olavo cleans
olavo washes
clear aquarium water
olavo clarifies
    olavo will retrieve
in aquarium water
olavo is adam
      olavo is eve
in the aquarium water
a fish winks
      olavo links
in the aquarium water
olavo scratches
    timing snatches
some orchard shadows
    on the headdress glows
frightened form rows
  to the sea the aquarium goes

•

draw

emanations of bards
penates, birds
psychiatric wards
what's in your cards?
charles the greats
marbles of marks
venus on mars
neither check nor mate

•

in the fields
at home
at the palace
on its last run
the last flower of latium

you cretin
you bronco
you clown
bid your final farewell
to the last flower of latium

by fire
by lasso
none can break the the fall
of the last flower of latium

●

tai-otoshi for kodokan gym

sluggish steps
write
DESIRE TO ARRIVE

it takes walking
like one already arrived

enough arriving already

quickly
is actually too slowly

following foot-trails with *footprints* footprints careful foot-trails barely *footprints* able foot-trails

footprints following *footprints* paring *footprints*

where *footprints* foot-trails pre- foot-trails i want foot-trails

without *footprints* foot-trails without *footprints* foot-trails as *footprints* sensed foot-trails as *footprints*

sensed foot-trails *footprints*

without foot-trails being

footprints

sigo picadas con *pegadas* cuidado picadas nal *pegadas* consigo picadas
por *pegadas* sigo picadas son *pegadas* pro picadas paro *pegadas*
son picadas ser *pegadas* sentido picadas cono *pegadas* cuero picadas
pegadas picadas *pegadas* picadas *pegadas*

SHOUT ROUTING BOUTS JUST THE SOUND STAYS AROUND

SH
HO
OU
UT
TT

SH
HO
OU
UT
TR
RO
OU
UT
TI
IN
NG
GB
BO
OU
UT
TS
SJ
JU
US
ST
TT
TH
HE
ES
SO
OU
UN
ND
DS
ST
TA
AY
YS
SA
AR
RO
OU
UN
ND
D

Translators' Afterword

Unencontraries and Beyond

While translating the complete poetry of Paulo Leminski we encountered constant reminders of his multiple interests and pursuits.[1] Literature, of course, was the primary one. He studied both classics and Modernisms (Anglo-American and Luso-Brazilian alike) and had a penchant for avant-garde writing. The expressive culture of Japan, including martial arts, was a lifelong passion. The four volumes by R. H. Blyth about the poetry of Nippon were on Leminski's bedside table for decades. He did many translations, including works by the joyous James Joyce, the Beat voice Lawrence Ferlinghetti, and John Lennon of The Beatles. The celebrated writer of Curitiba published quite a few reviews and essays concerning artistic topics, especially lyric. His range of concern is also seen in the biographies he wrote: the Messiah Jesus Christ, the ultimate revolutionary Leon Trotsky, the doyen of haiku Bashô, the black and foremost Brazilian symbolist poet Cruz e Sousa. Leminski was also deeply drawn to popular music; a dozen of the songs he composed (words and music) were recorded, as were four dozen of his lyrics set to music by others. He worked in journalism and advertising for years, putting to good use his sensibilities in graphic design and pithiness. And having pedagogical skills, he sometimes earned a living as a teacher-tutor for university prep courses. All of these activities are reflected in his variegated poetical endeavors.

Leminski's contributions both illustrate different paths of modern Brazilian poetry and enunciate a complex individual profile, a sui generis totality.[2] At age twenty, he published "inventions" in the vanguard arts journal of the renowned concrete poets in São Paulo, and he sustained an acute sense of visuality and typographic space in his output. He studied the forms and masters of haiku, a source ever in evidence. In the late 1970s and early 1980s his relaxed diction can be suggestive of the variously received trend of *poesia marginal*, although detached irony and language-based mini-texts set Leminski apart. In the late eighties formal rigor, abstraction, and intriguing imagery emerge with greater force. Although he confessed a desire to achieve communicability, his cosmopolitan poetical awareness manifests always. His frequent utilization of rhyme can evoke both song discourse and sublime symbolism. He was no stranger to paronomasia: puns, wordplay, linguistic gamesomeness, double entendre, rendering of which was one of the challenges of the present collection.

The spectrum of Leminski's poetry—from the straightforward to the erudite, from rock allusion to cosmic infusion, from the ordinary to the extraordinary—is broad, conciliatory, and multi-chromatic. The self-epigraph to *caprices and re-laxities* (p. 24) should be

[340]

read closely. The poems are characteristically brief and concise. He exhibits an abiding preference for quick phrasing and telegraphic economy in his bare verses, which may range, with deceptive simplicity, from the conversational, the commonplace, and the cute to the sophisticated, the obtuse, and the outright odd. His shortest piece is a single portmanteau word, and there are abundant poems of two to seven lines. In fact, of the 630 poems in this volume, over half (55%) are seven lines or less. Terms such as aphorism, distich, epigram, tercet, quatrain, ditty, doggerel, are all applicable throughout the collection. Because of this preponderance of restraint, longer poems such as "[the splendid steed]" (31 lines, p. 236) and "what's gone down, is gone down?" (57 lines, pp. 252-253) stand out more boldly.

As demonstrated by the rubrics *kawa cauim* (p. 199) and kawásu (p. 200), the division of three is special to Leminski, and entire sections of his books are dedicated to haiku, which is bonded to tertiary structure. In his repertories, the term is broadly conceived, including diverse haiku-like or haiku-related utterances, as he was never one to observe strict rules or definitions. The most important thing to him was the flavor and spirit of the Japanese model. In addition to the traditional employment of objective insightful observation of nature in haiku, there are pieces that one would call *senryu*, for their subjectivity or appeal to irony, satire, even humor. The Japanese term *haiga* for minimalist verse with a visual design or component also obtains.

As for vocabular and thematic paradigms, Leminski's preferences can be related to the common poetic spaces of haiku, or any sort of contemplative posture. Word searches return several repetitions and high counts of the corporeal (especially wings), the temporal (time-night-day-today-yesterday), the natural (wind, stone, flowers, shadow-shade), the aquatic (rain, sea, ocean, waves, shipwreck, teardrops), the celestial (moon, sun, sky, heaven, stars, clouds), extremes (the minimum, the maximum), and just plain life. There are sixty occurrences of poem / poetry / poet, which would amount to ten percent of the whole book if assigned one per poem.

Dialogue and intertextuality in Leminski's oeuvre can be subtle or explicit. There are direct references to such "difficult" authors as Mallarmé and Joyce, and serial excursions to the poetics of Bashô. Several of the considerable number of meta-literary poems here cite notable names of the Western tradition (e.g. Homer, Rimbaud, Pessoa, Ginsberg). Of particular note in this regard is the found-poem at the beginning of *La vie en close*, "boundaries unbound" (p. 214), a compilation of twenty-two quotes by Western poets/critics over the centuries about what poetry is, or not. One from Italian, two from Russian and Spanish, three from German, four from French and Portuguese, and six from English, a clear indication of how important Anglo-American references were for Leminski, who, incidentally, is the last phrasemaker revealingly cited: "the liberty of my language."

The poet's polyglot trajectory—he translated from thirteen languages—is further reflected in his own multi-lingual offerings. Seven poems here were originally written in English and two partially. There are two French items, one of which headlines his fourth book, and merits a dual translation (*La vie en close* alludes to the famous French song "La vie en rose" with a chopped French participle but also evinces English meanings, with voiced consonant, as in "close of business," or unvoiced, as in a cinematic close [up]). Readers will also see Polish, Japanese, Italian, Spanish, and Latin. This multilingual imperative established, it bears emphasizing that according to Leminski the Portuguese language forms the "substance of our [Brazilian] soul."

In a critical text about Latin, English and Portuguese, Leminski argued that the only strategy for Brazilians to resist cultural colonialism, the domination of Portuguese by English, would be to learn English. And that is what one of us did. The Brazilian concrete poets were also superb translators and critics. They argued that meticulous translating was the way to get to know a foreign text profoundly, and both of us have taken that notion to heart. We hope that Leminski's quality, expressive poetry will be as appreciated abroad as it has been at home, that it conquers the admiration of readers around the world via the present English renderings.

As for the title of this volume of translation, there are variations to consider. The very name of the source book, *Toda Poesia*, merits comment (it was chosen, by the way, by organizer Alice Ruiz and publisher Luiz Schwarcz, mentioned in the former's foreword). Portuguese-English dictionaries inform us that *todo* can mean *all, whole, every, entire, complete, total,* and by extension it can be *each, any,* or *collected.* A standard way to indicate "the collected poems / complete poetry" is *toda a poesia:* all the poetry. The absence of the article activates the phatic function of language: it calls attention to itself. The title *Toda Poesia* has two significant antecedents. One of the most representative Brazilian poets of the twentieth century, Ferreira Gullar (1930-2016), used it for the poems he collected when he turned fifty years old, but he continued writing for decades. Back in

1952, the entire lyrical catalogue of Brazil's foremost author of prose fiction was published as *Toda poesia de Machado de Assis*, an obscure volume today. Using this precise title for Leminski's life work proves to be a way to imply the poeticity of each and every item, aesthetic saturation, inclusivity, and totality. Any exaggeration or licentious extension should be accepted as part of the deal. Here, *All Poetry* is intended to convey both the adjectival and adverbial functions of the word *all*, and any others that might come forth.

Over the years, critical readers and admirers in Brazil have coined numerous nicknames for the creative writer-cultural agitator Paulo Leminski. Among the most suggestive are *samurai malandro*, the rogue urban hustler living by his wits and immersed in Japanese culture; *guerreiro lúdico*, gamesome warrior; and *anarquiteto de desengenharias*, anarchitect of disengineering. It would be great if after critically reading and admiring all the poems collected in the present volume some clever observer should craft an aptly imaginative moniker in the English language.

Charles A. Perrone and Ivan Justen Santana
July 2021

Notes

¹ The name of the multi-media exhibition about the artist that has toured Brazil since 2013 is precisely *Múltiplo Leminski*. For an English-language overview of the enterprise, see <https://multiploleminski.com.br/en/on-the-project/>.

² Coverage of Leminski in North America began with "PERHAPPINESS," critical preface, poems and translations, in *Brasil /Brazil: A Journal of Brazilian Literature* 7 (1992), 75-82; now available at the webspace of the academic co-sponsor: <https://repository.library.brown.edu/studio/item/bdr:918291/>. For wide context see Charles A. Perrone, *Seven Faces: Brazilian Poetry since Modernism* (Durham NC: Duke U P, 1996), esp. pp 141- 48 on Leminski. The title of the anthology *Nothing the Sun Could Not Explain: 20 Contemporary Brazilian Poets,* ed. Nelson Ascher, Régis Bonvicino and Michael Palmer (Los Angeles: Sun and Moon Press, 1997) is taken from the rendering of a poem by Leminski, who has several more items therein than any other poet. The title of this afterword is from the translation of a poem by Leminski whose title was used for the bi-lingual anthology *Desencontrários 6 poetas brasileiros / Unencontraries 6 Brazilian Poets* (Curitiba: Fundação Cultural-AC Avelino Vieira-Bamerindus, 1995), which, of course, included Leminski.

About the Translators

Charles A. Perrone is Professor Emeritus of Portuguese and Luso-Brazilian Culture and Literatures in the Department of Spanish and Portuguese Studies at the University of Florida. He is the author of *Letras e Letras da MPB* (1988, 2008), *Masters of Contemporary Brazilian Song: MPB 1965-1985* (1989), *Seven Faces: Brazilian Poetry since Modernism* (1996), and *Brazil, Lyric, and the Americas* (2010). In addition to edited volumes, articles and book chapters on Brazilian literature and popular music, he has translated numerous contemporary Brazilian poets and writers. His first translations of Paulo Leminski date from the early 1990s. He now lives in Santa Cruz, California.

Ivan Justen Santana is a teacher-scholar-translator. He was born in 1973, in Curitiba, capital of the state of Paraná, the same city where Paulo Leminski was born and worked. Ivan never had the chance to meet the poet in person, since he passed away in 1989, but has studied his work for decades. Ivan has a B.A. in English language and literature from the Federal University of Paraná (UFPR), a Master´s degree in Translation Studies from the University of São Paulo (with a thesis on the translations made by Leminski), and a Ph. D in Literary Studies from the UFPR.

New London Librarium

New London Librarium is a boutique press that specializes in books that merit publication but which are unlikely to reach sales levels expected by larger publishers. Many of NLL's titles relate to the culture, literature, history, and current issues relating to Brazil. Other series focus on history, Catholic issues, fiction, and art. Among translations are works by Machado de Assis, Rubem Alves, Mário de Andrade, Paulo Leminski, Monteiro Lobato, and João do Rio. For more information, see NLLibrarium.com.

www.ingramcontent.com/pod-product-compliance
Lightning Source LLC
Chambersburg PA
CBHW022004080426
42733CB00007B/463